OREGON HIGH

A CLIMBING GUIDE TO NINE CASCADE VOLCANOES

MT. HOOD
MT. JEFFERSON
THREE FINGERED JACK
MT. WASHINGTON
THREE SISTERS
BROKEN TOP
MT. THIELSEN

by
JEFF THOMAS

KEEP CLIMBING PRESS

To my mother
Betty Jane Paxton Thomas
(1919-1985)

Keep Climbing Press
Portland, Oregon

Manufactured in the United States of America
Cover photo by Jay Carroll, Photo/Grafix. Climbers approaching Leuthold
Couloir, Mt.Hood. Yocum Ridge in background.
Backcover photo by Alan Kearney. Climber on Eliot Glacier Headwall, Mt.
Hood.
Book and cover design by Jay and Muki Kerr, K2 Graphics
Editors Karen Lewis and Talbot Bielefeldt

I.S.B.N. # 0-9629042-0-1

Bill Thomas on The Crawl, Three Fingered Jack　　　*Jeff Thomas photo*

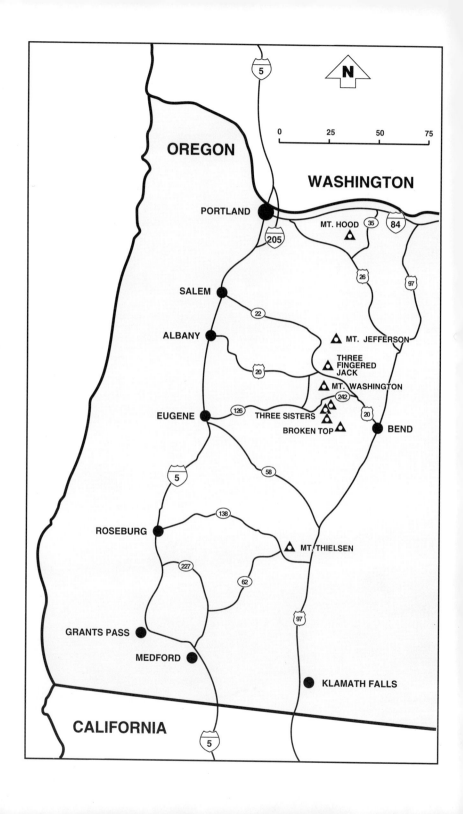

CONTENTS

ACKNOWLEDGMENTS

Speaking from experience, extracting information from climbers is often like pulling teeth, until after the thing is published, then everyone turns out to be an expert.
Jim Ramsey on writing a climbing guide

Stu Stuller started this project in 1981, then dropped it to work for *Outside*. I have been trying to finish ever since. Vera Dafoe, Phil Jones, and Jim Ramsey have encouraged and helped me in many ways. My father has dragged me off to the mountains where all guidebook authors must go to write successfully. Nick Dodge allowed me to look over his notes for two previous Oregon Climbing Guides. John Chunn was kind enough to share his intimate knowledge about Broken Top. Hank Lewis and Al Monner allowed me to look through the archives of the Wy'east Climbers. Brian Johnson, great grandson of John B. Waldo, contributed to my knowledge of Judge Waldo. Jim Blanchard was instrumental in allowing me to see the papers of Gary Leech. The Mazamas allowed me access to their summit registers and gave me a generous research grant. Lois Schreiner helped me find Obsidian documents. Other people who helped with the manuscript are Peter Green, Jim Lathrop, Laurita Leuthold, Bo Nonn, and David Schermer. Don Lowe and Terry Toedtemeier have significantly added to the quality of this book with their photos. Jay Kerr was indispensable during the production phase of this monster. Finally, I would like to acknowledge Tom Bauman, for his help on the Mt. Washington and Three Sisters chapters.

AUTHOR'S NOTE

While working on *Oregon Rock*, I became fascinated with the history of climbing in the mountains and crags of Oregon. Between 1983 and 1990, I spent at least one month a year interviewing old timers and visiting archives, trying to trace forgotten climbs and climbers. The research was used to develop a manuscript which was a combination climbing guide and climbing history. Space restrictions and the marketplace forced me to drop most of the climbing history. Thus, *Oregon High* is primarily a guidebook. Still, I hope enough color has crept into the first ascent data to capture the imaginations of those who enjoy more than the dry prose of a route description. If this book is a success, I will publish the second and perhaps more interesting half of the original manuscript. Meanwhile, if the background of a particular climb intrigues you, use the references and the Bibliography to find out more. Finally, I would appreciate hearing about any omissions or corrections, which are inevitable in a project of this size. I am also interested in three routes, for which I could not find route descriptions: The Black Spider on Mt. Hood, a direct route up Castle Crags on Mt. Hood, and the North Cleaver between Jefferson Park Glacier and Russell Glacier on Mt. Jefferson. Call me at 503-232-3899.

During the life time of men now living, the greater part of this inhabitable continent has been given into private hands. 'The end of the land' has been reached....An urgent need of the hour would seem to be, not more land to cultivate, but some change for the better in our ideas....There are educational uses in mountains and the wilderness which might well justify a wise people in preserving and reserving them for such uses; and such a people might find this (Cascade Range Forest) reservation not only wisely reserved, but to be none too great a tract for such a purpose. Why should not Americans, with a continent in their hands to fashion as they would, have provided broadly for all the needs of men which can be supplied?...Not only fields to toil in, but mountains and wilderness to camp in, to hunt and fish in, and where, in communion with untrammeled nature and the free air, the narrowing tendencies of an artificial and petty existence might be perceived and corrected, and the spirit enlarged and strengthened.

John B. Waldo to President Grover Cleveland in 1896

INTRODUCTION

WARNING

Oregon High is a climbing guide, not a hiking or technical scrambling guide. To climb safely, you must know how to: use crampons, self-arrest, and belay on snow or ice; set up a crevasse rescue; and anchor, belay, and rappel on rock. If you do not have these minimum skills, **stop here and do not use this book.** Climbing in the mountains is hazardous. To learn how to climb safely, seek instruction from a knowledgeable friend, a local climbing club or a climbing school.

If you know how to climb, use the information in these pages cautiously. Climbing guides are not Bibles. Training, instinct and judgement should prevail whenever you make a climbing decision. Climb at your own risk.

OVERVIEW

Oregon High is a climbing guide to Mount Hood, Mount Jefferson, Three Fingered Jack, Mount Washington, North Sister, Middle Sister, South Sister, Broken Top, and Mount Thielsen. All nine mountains are dormant or dead volcanoes in the high Cascades of Oregon, which have been eroded in varying degrees by glaciation. As you will quickly discover, easier climbs follow gentler slopes which have not been heavily glaciated, or low-angle ridges left standing between glaciers. Generally these easier routes can be safely climbed throughout the year. More difficult climbing can be found on the steep headwalls of glacial cirques. The rock forming these headwalls is the stuff nightmares are made of, volcanic junk that would just as soon collapse as it would stand. This rock must be covered by consolidated snow or ice if you want to avoid avalanches, rockfall, and scary if not life threatening rock climbing.

The nine mountains in this book are not destination climbing centers. There are no "classic climbs" or "latest rages" that can be checked off your fifty most wanted list. However, the particular mix of mild but wet winters and generally poor rock creates its own challenge, which can be as rewarding as climbing in other, more sought-after ranges. Parties willing to wait for the right combination of conditions will be rewarded with moderate to difficult alpine climbing. Ski mountaineers will find a number of challenging ascents and descents, especially in the Three Sisters area. In addition, mountains like Hood, Jefferson and the Three Sisters appeal to more people because they are easier to climb than a Grand Teton or a Mt. McKinley. The appeal is further enhanced by the dominance of each summit over its surrounding territory and the location of each mountain, either wholly or partially within wilderness boundaries. The majority of climbs in this book, although requiring technical skill and know-how, place a greater emphasis on physical fitness and general outdoor skills.

STAYING ALIVE

In North America, roughly 60 people die in mountaineering and back country accidents each year. But the question still remains, how dangerous is mountaineering? What are the chances of being hurt or killed? According to a report quoted in the American Alpine Club's *Accidents in North American Mountaineering*, experts, who base their results on fatality statistics, were asked to rank the risks of dying from various activities and technologies. Mountain climbing came in 29th, behind such activities as operating a power mower, school football, using contraceptives, police work, and surgery.

Still, it is the opinion of many professional and volunteer rescue organizations that most accidents in North America are the result of ignorance, impulsiveness, and irresponsibility. People who educate themselves as to the potential hazards, equip themselves accordingly, and act responsibly, rarely have difficulty. A thorough discussion of safety is beyond the scope of this book, but in the spirit of every educational plug helps, here are some guidelines to follow while climbing Oregon volcanoes. (See also *Mountaineering: The Freedom of the Hills* by the Mountaineers and *Wilderness Search and Rescue* by Tim J. Setnicka).

The most challenging aspect of climbing mountains anywhere in the world is the speed at which the weather changes. Many climbers do not plan for poor weather and are caught ill-prepared. As a result, the number-one factor in mountaineering accidents is hypothermia. This is especially true in the Pacific Northwest, because temperatures often hover between 28 and 40 degrees and precipitation is usually cold rain or wet snow. Ironically, many of Oregon's worst accidents occur when bad weather catches a party on low angle slopes such as the gentle South Side of Mt. Hood. This so-called "easy" route has trapped uncounted climbers, and killed more individuals than any other climb on the mountain. The most recent calamity, where nine members of the Oregon Episcopal School died in May of 1986, is the worst but by no means only example. Similar tragedies have occurred on the South Side in 1927, 1938 and 1969.

The upshot is that you must plan for the worst. Wear wool or synthetic clothing and take waterproof jacket and pants. Carry map, compass, watch, and consider carrying an altimeter. Use these tools to gauge your progress and know whether it is time to turn around. Be prepared for an emergency bivouac with matches, extra food, stove, and emergency shelter.

Except for Mt. Washington, avoid climbing rock when you can. All Cascade rock is volcanic and most of it is bad. It is so terrifying that it is often treated as a joke. Comments such as, "slag heap," "this whole mountain was swept out of a cow barn," "can't someone staple these rocks down" and, "how long will it last" are common in the old summit registers. The all-time winner is the following one-liner by Nick Dodge, written in the Broken Top register after he climbed a route on the north side of the mountain. "We are sure what we climbed was buried last year and will be gone next year." Outward Bound instructors, who, while teaching in the Three Sisters, became familiar with the nature of the rock, came up with the term

Introduction

"Oregon Death Tours" to label a group of some of the more hideous climbs. Standing underneath exposed rock is as dangerous as climbing on it, as the following incident illustrates. The climb was Cooper Spur. The climber, Lige Coalman. The time was September 1917.

> *He was startled by a roar above him that sounded as if the top of the mountain had broken loose. He jerked off his glasses...and looked up to see what was happening. A large segment of a 200-foot ledge had broken loose 2000 feet above. It came hurtling down. There was no protection; no place to run. The whole mass disintegrated into fragments that leaped high, bounced sideways, or came straight forward like cannon balls. There were stones varying from the size of a walnut to boulders weighing more than a ton. It did not seem possible that any living thing could survive. Lige committed himself to his Maker and prayed. (White 1972)*

Lige Coalman miraculously survived. Although an extreme example, his story illustrates why you should wear a helmet on even the easiest routes.

Because volcanic rock is so unstable, you must climb when it is buried by snow or frozen in place. In general, May and June have the best combination of stable weather, low freezing level, and snow cover. Fall and winter occasionally produce excellent conditions. If you are looking for the elusive but ever-hoped-for water ice, this is when you will find it. Although the weather is almost universally good in July, August, and sometimes September, the mountains are bare of snow, and the freezing level fluctuates rapidly. Avoid climbing in summer unless you plan to do one of the lower angle routes or your route follows a ridgeline. No matter what time of year it is, avoid climbing in the late afternoon. Start early and finish early. Early starts mean easier, more efficient walking, climbing with less rockfall, and earlier, safer descents on firmer snow. Early starts also allow more time to resolve problems and conduct rescues.

Oregon glaciers are small, but size is no measure of danger. Follow standard procedure and rope up whenever crossing a glacier.

Eighty to ninety percent of all avalanches occur during or within 24 hours after a storm. You must be wary of the 10 to 20 percent which are triggered long after the storm has passed. Generally these occur on slopes of 25 to 45 degrees, on the leeward side of a ridge where large cornices and drifts form. Well known areas where these conditions occur include the slopes above West Crater Rim, the lower slopes of Wy'east, the East Face of Mt. Jefferson, and the east side of the South Ridge of Three Fingered Jack. Read as much as you can about avalanches. Two books to start off with are *The ABC of Avalanche Safety* by Edward R. LaChapelle and *Avalanche Safety for Skiers & and Climbers* by Tony Daffern. Further information can be obtained from a USFS brochure, *Avalanche Safety Information for Washington and Northern Oregon* or from the USFS Northwest Avalanche Center in Portland at 503-326-2400.

A rare but deadly hazard in Oregon is lightning. The summit of Mt. Jefferson has seen one lightning-strike death in recent time, and Mt. Thielsen is often called the lightning rod of Oregon. An abundance of fulgurite (rock fused by lightning) on top of both pinnacles proves that strikes are not uncommon. There have also been close calls on Mt. Hood and the Three Sisters.

AMS (acute mountain sickness) often occurs above 8,000 feet, and is a frequent problem for Cascade peak climbers who go from sea level to summit too quickly.

Finally, it has been observed that accidents occur over and over in the same places. Take extra care if you are descending the top 1,000 feet of Cooper Spur on Mt. Hood, traversing the west-side snowfield under the The Pinnacle of Mt. Jefferson, or traversing the west-side snowfield under Prouty Pinnacle on North Sister. These three areas have seen a high percentage of fatalities.

CLIMB RATINGS

Guidebooks have traditionally used a system of hierarchical numbers and letters to rate climbing difficulty. In Europe the system is called the Union Internationale des Associations D'Alpinisme, or UIAA. In North America the Yosemite Decimal System (YDS) has gained the widest acceptance. While similar overall, both systems differ in particulars. Neither method is an effective way of rating snow climbs, which can change in difficulty overnight.

Since the majority of climbs in Oregon are snow climbs, most of the routes in this book are not graded. Instead, when known, each route description contains information on the steepest pitch climbed, the average time required to get from one point to another, and any special dangers which may exist.

The average time of ascent is based on summit register entries and an informal survey of climbers. Many parties and individuals will be able to improve on these times, which may add to their safety margin. Those who fall significantly behind should carefully consider turning around at the first sign of unstable weather.

The maximum angle on a given climb or pitch is based on estimates gathered from other climbers. Estimates are notoriously inaccurate, but most climbers are not inclined to whip out a clinometer while struggling up the crux pitch. Where opinions differ, this book leans toward the higher figure.

Rock climbing difficulty is rated according to the Yosemite Decimal System, which uses the numbers 1 through 5:

1. Trail hiking.
2. Scrambling over talus or through brush.
3. Steep slopes or exposed ridges.
4. Steep rock requiring a rope but no further gear.
5. Roped climbing and belays.

Class 5 is further broken down to measure the most difficult free move on a roped climb. A decimal point and the numbers 1 through 14 are used. For example, a 5.1 climb is relatively easy and can be done by most people in good physical condition, while a 5.14 climb is extremely difficult and is seldom climbed successfully. There are no rock climbs in this book harder than 5.10.

WILDERNESS ETHICS AND REGULATIONS

Climbers as a whole are quite well educated about the delicate nature of the sub-alpine environment and about methods of low impact camping. This does not seem to stop many individuals from modifying their ethics and camping in places that suit their climbing plans rather than behaving in ways that ensure the lowest possible environmental impact. Do not lose site of the importance of preserving delicate wild areas just so you can save a few minutes' climbing in the morning. Use common sense, and remember that Forest Service regulations prohibit the following in all Oregon wilderness areas.

1. **Fire:** Building, maintaining, attending or using a campfire within 100 foot slope distance of any permanent lake, stream, spring, pond or trail system.
2. **Mechanized Equipment:** Possessing or using bicycles, wagons, carts or wheelbarrows (except wheelchairs).
3. **Rehabilitated Sites:** Camping or being within areas posted as closed for rehabilitation.
4. **Motorized Equipment:** Possessing or using a motorized vehicle or motorized equipment.
5. **Trees and Vegetation:** Cutting or damaging any timber tree or other forest product except as authorized.
6. **Sanitation:** Littering, leaving debris in an exposed or unsanitary condition or placing in a stream or lake any substance which causes pollution.
7. **Groups:** Groups larger than 12 persons and 12 head of stock without a permit.

The Forest Service also has specific regulations that apply to special areas within each wilderness. See the chapters on each mountain for more details.

The Forest Service recommends several techniques to help preserve the wilderness for everyone's enjoyment.

1. **Travel to avoid impacts.** Do not cut switchbacks, and avoid making new or multiple trails.
2. **Make No-Trace Camps.** Avoid compacted and heavily used camp sites. Choose well-drained, rocky, sandy, or timbered locations 200 feet from lakes and streams. Do not trample or remove vegetation. Refrain from leveling tent sites. Use gas stoves whenever possible.
3. **Water.** Protect the water resource by washing at least 200 feet away from water sources using biodegradable soaps, and keeping food stuffs out of lakes and streams.
4. **Human Waste.** If possible carry out solid waste and toilet paper, otherwise bury 6 inches deep.
5. **Litter.** Pack out all trash: yours and others. Remember tin foil will not burn, and animals will dig up buried garbage.

FOREST SERVICE WILDERNESS PERMITS

The Forest Service has announced plans to begin a permit system in the Mt. Jefferson Wilderness, the Mt. Washington Wilderness, and Three Sisters Wilderness. A fee will be charged to cover the costs of administration. The system will be implemented in two phases beginning in 1991. The first phase of the permit system will be mandatory, but numbers will not be restricted. Permits will be required for both day and overnight users.

The second phase of the permit would be a regulatory permit system that would limit the number of people entering the wilderness. A regulatory permit might be required as early as 1992. It could be specific to key impact areas, and not encompass the whole Wilderness. Options that will be considered are: utilizing regulatory permits only during peak use periods; including regulation by travel zone or trailheads; issuing permits on first come, first served basis or by reservations, or a mixture of both, etc. (USFS 1990).

The American Alpine Club has appealed the Forest Service plan. The Forest Service will not reach a decision on the appeal until after this book is printed.

ABBREVIATIONS, DIRECTIONS, AND PHOTO KEY

Directions are given as if the climber were facing the cliff or snow slope. The following abbreviations are used throughout this book:

3FJ	Three Fingered Jack summit register	
BT	Broken Top summit register	
FA	first ascent	
FD	first descent	
FFA	first free ascent	
FRA	first recorded ascent	
FWA	first winter ascent	
H	Mt. Hood summit register	
Ill	Illumination Rock summit Register	
J	Mt. Jefferson summit register	
MS	Middle Sister summit register	
NS	North Sister summit register	
PCT	Pacific Crest Trail	
SS	South Sister summit register	
T	Mt. Thielsen summit register	
USFS	United States Forest Service	
USGS	United States Geodetic Survey	
W	Mt. Washington summit register	

PHOTO KEY

CLIMBING ROUTE

—·—·—·—·—·—·—
ROUTE VARIATION

·················
ROUTE OBSCURED

Jon Dasler just after the Third Gendarme rappel, Yocum Ridge   *John Smolich photo*

MT. HOOD (11,239')

That night, hardly anyone in camp would say that they wished ever to ascend Mt. Hood again. After a nights rest several of us thought we might be willing sometime; and before we had gone halfway home every member of the party had made some plan to climb again.

Anon

DESCRIPTION

Mt. Hood lies just south of the Columbia River and about 50 air miles east of Portland, Oregon. It is the highest mountain in Oregon, and its height is further accentuated by its striking beauty and dominant position above the Columbia River. Mt. Hood is so prominent and well known that its image is used to represent everything from the commercial to the sublime.

As anyone who has climbed the South Side of the mountain knows, Mt. Hood is a dormant, not a dead volcano. Signs of recent volcanic activity are everywhere. Geologist say that some of this activity occurred about 200 years ago between 1760 and 1810, producing ashflows, mudflows, lava, and at least one pyroclastic flow. All of these events apparently originated from vents just above Crater Rock in the areas known as Devils Kitchen and Hot Rocks. Because thermal activity continues around these areas to this day, geologists believe that molten magma is still present beneath Mt. Hood, and that further activity is very likely.

The most likely eruptive event in the future will be the formation of another dome, probably within the present south-facing crater. The principal hazards that could accompany dome formation include pyroclastic flows and mudflows moving from the upper slopes of the volcano down the floors of valleys. (Crandell 1980)

Future geologic hazards are not the only threat to today's climber. Geologists say that of the major Northwest volcanoes, only Mt. St. Helens has a higher percentage of pyroclastics. Pyroclastics are loosely compacted fragmental material formed during an explosive eruption. Climbing on pyroclastics is similar to climbing on vertical rubble, you are never sure what is going to pull loose and what else it will bring down on top of you. Most of this type of rock is concentrated in the upper 4,000 feet of Mt. Hood, ample explanation for why Mt. Hood is not known for rock climbing.

Mt. Hood

A huge glacier smothered Mt. Hood during the last ice age, and probably removed at least 1,000 feet from the top of the mountain. Scars on trees lining the Eliot Glacier show that current glaciers on the north side of Mt. Hood were surging forward as late as 1740 (Lawrence 1958). In the 1890s the Eliot was still extensive enough that ice could be collected conveniently by the proprietors of Cloud Cap Inn to refrigerate food. Glaciers on the South Side of Mt. Hood were also advancing in the recent pass. In a report on glaciers of the Pacific Slope, Arnold Hague described the White River Glacier as,

> *nearly a quarter of a mile wide at the head, and about two miles long, extending 500 feet below the line of timber-growth upon the sides of the mountain.* (King, C. 1871)

Today, the 11 named glaciers on Mt. Hood are retreating, probably as a result of a world-wide warming trend. Warmer weather has also reduced the amount of permanent snow, as the following two witnesses attest.

> *Left Cloud Cap Inn at 7:15 Aug. 27th 1895. Party consisting of H.L. Pittock, etc....Mr. Pittock was the pioneer of the party having made the ascension in 1857, 1858, and 1859. He notices no change in the mountain except that there is much less snow on the peak than in the early days.* (H 1895)

> *The change that impressed me most (aside from automobile access) was the reduction in snow cover on Mt. Jefferson and Mt. Hood. In 1905 on Mt. Hood when we were camped at timberline, the snow in the valleys between the rocky ridges was virtually at timberline in August. The climb to Crater Rock from timberline was on snow.* (Montgomery, W. 1984)

Despite poor rock and a diminishing snowbase, Mt Hood has the right mix of accessibility, altitude, and variety. The mountain is easily reached without the burden of organizing a major expedition. It is high enough to test your abilities at altitude but low enough to be descend quickly in an emergency. The variety of routes and snow conditions, if approached intelligently, gradually expose the aspiring alpinist to the hard lessons of mountaineering.

<u>MAPS</u>

There are currently (1991) five maps available for Mt. Hood and vicinity. The two 7.5-minute USGS maps are not as useful as they might be because each map only shows half of the mountain.

1. Mt. Hood North, 7.5 minute quadrangle, published by USGS in 1980
2. Mt. Hood South, 7.5 minute quadrangle, published by USGS in 1980.

3. Mt. Hood and Vicinity, published by USGS in 1984. This map shows Hood and vicinity in 24,000 scale and 100,000 scale.
4. Mt. Hood Wilderness, published by the USFS in 1983.
5. Geo-Graphics Mt. Hood Wilderness Map, and Columbia Gorge and Mt. Hood Recreation Map, published 1990 by Geo-Graphics of Portland, OR.

ROADS AND TRAILS

Timberline Road. Timberline Road leads to Timberline Lodge (roughly 5,960 feet), and provides the best year-round access to routes on the west, south, and southeast sides of the mountain. In winter, some climbers even use Timberline to approach climbs on the north side. Drive to Government Camp on U.S. Highway 26. About four-tenths of a mile past the eastern leg of the Government Camp Loop road, turn left on the Timberline road, and drive about six miles to the Lodge parking area. Climbers can self-register 24 hours a day in a protected area just outside Timberline's Wy'east Day Lodge. The day lodge is on the west side of the upper end of the parking area. When registering, climbers can also listen to a 24 hour weather forecast on radio, broadcast by the National Weather Service.

Cooper Spur Road and Cloud Cap Road (USFS 3512). These two roads lead to Tilly Jane Campground, Cloud Cap Saddle Campground, and Cloud Cap Inn (roughly 5,920 feet). They are not plowed during the winter, and generally can only be driven from June to late October or early November. When open, they are the most convenient access for north-side routes.

Follow State Highway 35 about 23 miles from Hood River, or follow U.S. 26 and State Highway 35 about 20 miles from Government Camp. Turn west onto the Cooper Spur Road and drive about 2.5 miles to the Cooper Spur Ski Area road. Turn left and follow the road for less than a mile. At the first fork, stay right. At the second fork take the right unpaved fork (the left fork goes to the parking area for Cooper Spur Ski area) and drive about nine miles to Cloud Cap Inn. Several hundred yards before Cloud Cap Inn, park at a small USFS campground called Cloud Cap Saddle.

Cooper Spur Ski Trail (USFS 643). Cooper Spur Ski Trail is often used in winter or early spring to approach north-side climbs. Leave the car at a Sno Park just below Cooper Spur Ski Area (see Cloud Cap Road for approach) where Cloud Cap Road (USFS 3512) begins its nine-mile climb. The trail begins less than 100 feet up Cloud Cap Road and leads to Tilly Jane Campground (5,718 feet), which is a short distance from Cloud Cap Inn. Total distance from the ski area to Cloud Cap is about three miles.

Cooper Spur Ski Trail is steep enough that many nordic skiers choose to descend Cloud Cap Road. Use shortcuts to shorten the trip down the road, including Ghost Ridge and an old telephone line right of way. For further information see *Cross Country Ski Routes of Oregon's Cascades* by Klindt Vielbig.

USFS 1825, 1828, 118, Top Spur Trail (USFS 785), and McNeil Point. Follow this route in late spring, summer, and fall to approach the west side of Mt. Hood. Follow U.S. 26 to Zigzag, a small town 18 miles east of Sandy. Turn north on Lolo Pass Road and drive 4.4 miles toward Lolo pass. Where the road forks, turn right on USFS 1825 and drive 0.6 miles toward McNeil Campground and Ramona Falls. Turn left on USFS 1828 just before 1825 crosses a bridge over the Sandy River. Drive 5.8 miles on paved roadway. At a fork in the road, stay right on unpaved USFS 118, and follow it 1.6 miles to the Top Spur Trail.

Park in a wide spot in USFS Road 118. Cross the road and follow the unsigned but obvious Top Spur Trail, up the cut bank and into the woods. Hike less than half a mile to the intersection with the PCT. Go south on the PCT for less than a minute, and turn left up Bald Mountain Ridge toward Cairn Basin (USFS 600). Follow the Ridge for about an hour (excellent views of Mt. Hood). At the top of four short switchbacks, leave the main trail and follow an unsigned but obvious trail through a large meadow and onto a steep ridge trail. Continue up to the stone shelter at McNeil Point. Total distance from the roadhead to the shelter is approximately 4 miles.

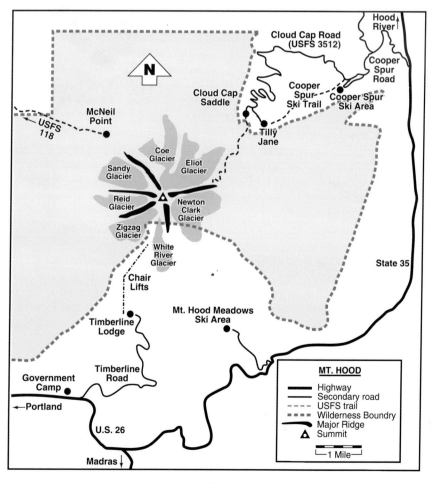

DESCENT

The South Side is the only recommended descent from the summit of Mt. Hood in an emergency or a storm. Portland Mountain Rescue distributes a two-page brochure on how to get down the South Side in low-visibility conditions. Anyone climbing Mt. Hood should read and understand this brochure.

CLIMBERS BEWARE THE MT. HOOD TRIANGLE.

Most search and rescue operations on Mt. Hood are the result of climbers becoming lost on their descent from the South Side Route. Others have become lost while descending from camps at Illumination Saddle.

The most common problem occurs when visibility becomes poor and climbers descend without aid of map and compass, thinking that if they simply go back downhill they will surely return to the lodge.

However, the fall line (route a ball will take if let roll down a slope) from the base of Crater Rock down to about the elevation of the top of the Palmer Ski Lift, does not fall toward Timberline Lodge on the south, but rather, southwesterly in the direction of the Zigzag Canyon and the cliffs of Mississippi Head.

An area of the descent that has caused a number of people to become confused and lost, is the traverse around the east slopes of the base of Crater Rock. Occasionally, a climber will drop too low on the traverse and descend into the White River Glacier and canyon to the east of the route.

More often, climbers will traverse around Crater Rock, staying on the correct descent route, but then glissade down the fall line to the westerly, unaware they are in trouble until they reach the canyons or cliffs below.

Carry a map and compass. Use your compass and believe it. Once you have descended around Crater Rock, it can be noted that by simply following the direction of the southerly end of the magnetic compass needle you will descend very close to the ski lifts and Silcox Hut. In low visibility the descent by your compass may seem strange in that you will find yourself sidehilling considerably to the left as you descend from Crater Rock to below 9,000 feet.

Cooper Spur is sometimes used as a descent route after a north side climb. However many who are familiar with Cooper Spur, choose to descend the South Side. See the Cooper Spur route description for more details.

ROUTES

1 South Side

Pundits claim that the South Side of Mt. Hood is the most-climbed mountain route in the world, with the exception of Mt. Fuji in Japan. To anyone who has climbed the South Side on a good weekend in May or June, this claim seems to be irrefutable fact. The mountain is crowded, and getting from the top of the Hogback to the summit often requires waiting in line.

According to the latest USFS records (1985), somewhere between 10,000 and 14,000 individuals climb Mt. Hood every year. The USFS also states that these numbers do not accurately reflect the actual number of people on the mountain, because many parties choose not to sign in. Although there are no official estimates, most of the people who climb Mt. Hood climb the South Side.

Many climbers also believe that the South Side is an easy climb which can be done by senior citizens carrying 200-pound packs and preschoolers unaccompanied by their mommies or daddies. The written record does show that in the right conditions, almost anyone can slog up this route. Over the years many couples have climbed the South Side and been married on the summit. Ivan Woolley states in *Off To Mt. Hood,*

> *Upon two occasions the Knights of Columbus engaged Ray Conway to guide parties from their lodge up the mountain and each time Ray packed an altar on his back all the way to the top so that mass could be held on the summit.*

Material to build a fire lookout was packed up the South Side by the USFS in 1916. When the lookout finally collapsed in the forties, a group of Crag Rats hauled loads of powdered rubber from recapped tires to the summit and set the remains on fire. Ty and Marianna (Sinclair) Kearney and their party packed a bicycle up the South Side and rode it along the summit ridge in 1947. The South Side has been climbed by blind people and people without limbs. At least two five-year-old children have climbed the south side under their own steam. Uncounted senior citizens, some in their eighties, have reached the summit. Fiftieth anniversary climbs are not uncommon and one gentleman, Hank Lewis, made his 64th anniversary climb in 1986. A dog, Ranger, holds the record for the most ascents of the South Side, estimated at over a 1,000 (Blanchard 1985). When he died, his body was packed up the South Side and buried on the summit. Wild animals, including bear and deer, have also been observed climbing or descending the South Side.

Ironically, the gentle, broad slopes which are so simple to climb in good weather become a windy, whited-out hell in bad weather. Trapped on the South Side in such conditions, it matters little whether you can ace 5.14 on sight or downclimb vertical rime ice backwards. Climbing is reduced to the basics of navigation and

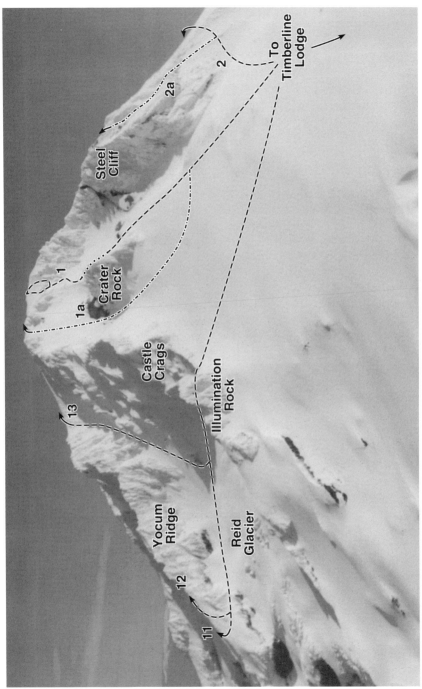

Mt Hood from the Southwest

Bill Bryan photo

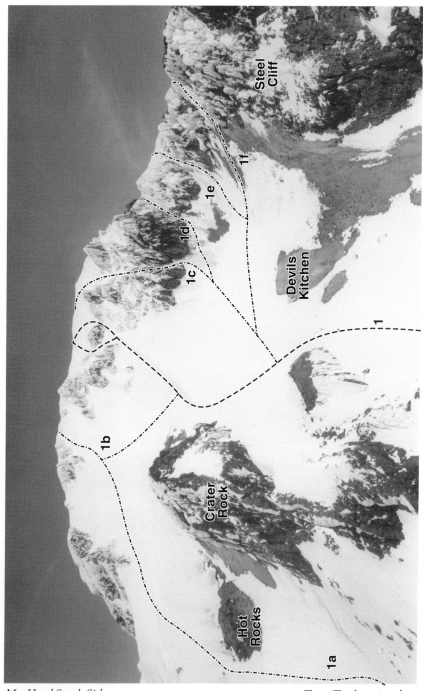

Mt. Hood South Side   *Terry Toedtemeier photo*

survival. Anyone planning to climb Mt. Hood must be familiar with the South Side and how to get down it in a storm (see Descent).

Start on the east side of Timberline lodge. Do not follow the groomed ski trails; instead stay east in the trees and hike one mile to Silcox warming hut (approx. 7,000 feet). Continue another mile to the end of the Palmer ski lift (approx. 8,600 feet). From the end of the ski lift, climb toward the right or east side of Crater Rock, then continue around and up the east side of the rock to the Hogback (approx. 10,600 feet), a high ridge of snow extending from the north side of Crater Rock toward the summit. Follow the Hogback to a large bergschrund. Cross or go around the bergschrund, depending on conditions. Enter a gully, commonly called the Chute, which leads through several rock towers (The Pearly Gates) to the summit ridge. Time from Timberline Lodge, 6-10 hours.

FA: W.L Chittenden, James G. Dierdorff (one newspaper spells it Deardorff), W.L. Buckley, L.J. Powell, and Henry L. Pittock, Aug. 6, 1857. According to an account written by James G. Dierdorff in 1857, the party had to traverse 100 yards west under the bergschrund in order to find a snow bridge. Pittock further stated in an article published in 1864 that upon gaining the summit ridge they discovered that one more step would plunge them down the awesome north side. Taken together, the two statements indicate the party used what is now referred to as the Old Chute (see variations).

Record time Government Camp to summit and back, 3 hours 14 minutes and 3 seconds, Steve Boyer, August 1984 (Lee 1984).

Variation 1A: West Crater Rim. West Crater Rim was called the Zigzag Glacier Route in the 1930s. Zigzag Glacier Route is more appropriate because the route does not actually gain the west crater rim, but it is difficult to change a name once it has become established. On busy days, West Crater Rim is less crowded than the South Side. Move around the left (west) side of Crater Rock. Climb a steep slope to the left of the Hot Rocks, and gain a shelf of snow on the western side of the Crater. Move North to the base of the Old Chute and follow it to the summit rim. Turn east and follow the rim to the top.

Be aware that this route is directly in the path of debris falling off Crater Rock, and of any avalanche coming off the slopes above Castle Crags. Huge slides are not uncommon during or right after heavy snowfall, and sometimes in Spring. If conditions are at all shaky, avoid this route. **FA:** unknown.

Variation 1B: Old Chute. Photographs taken at the turn of the century show the Hogback in the position it is found in today. Photographs taken during the 1920s, 1930s, 1940s, and 1950s show the Hogback shifted sharply to the west and significantly reduced in size. Sometime during the 1960s the Hogback again shifted east to its current position and grew in size.

In the 1930s, the gully which led from the top of the Hogback to the summit became known as the Chute. When the Hogback shifted back toward the east in the 1960s, climbers followed it and started to use a different gully to gain the summit. Although the route was different, it was still called the Chute. To distinguish between the two, the term Old Chute means the route on the west.

If the bergschrund is impassable, or the Chute is jammed with people, try the

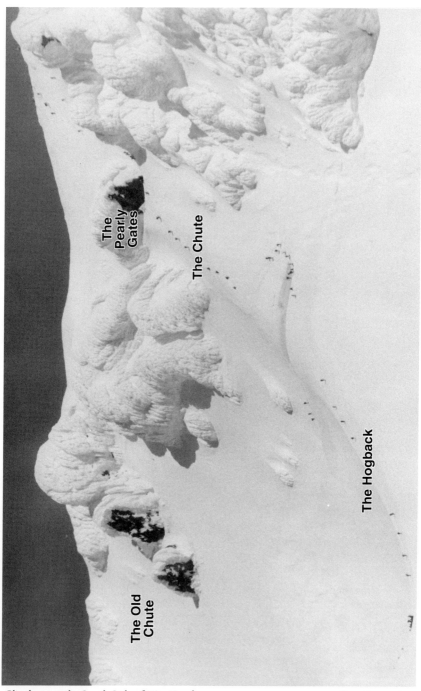

Climbers on the South Side of Mt. Hood   *Don Lowe photo*

Old Chute. From the Hogback, climb diagonally up and left onto a steep face which leads to the summit ridge. Turn right and follow the ridge to the top. When you reach the top of the Old Chute, do not be surprised by the narrowness of the ridgetop and the sharp drop down the north face.

FA: see first ascent of South Side.

Variation 1C & 1D: Devils Kitchen Headwall. Avoid Devils Kitchen Headwall unless it is covered by ice and snow. It is relatively easy under winter conditions, the maximum angle being somewhere between 55 and 60 degrees. Start from the Hogback and traverse right above Devils Kitchen. Climb the headwall, using one of several gullies.

FA: unknown. Devils Kitchen Headwall may have been climbed August 15, 1900 by George and Fred Schwartz, two Swiss immigrants. An article appearing in the Oregonian gave some details of their climb, but not enough to say with certainty that they climbed the headwall.

Variation 1E: Flying Buttress. Near the upper left side of Steel Cliff, a buttress runs obliquely from the bottom of the face to the top of the rim. Climb the buttress to gain the east crater rim. The buttress was popular in the 1930s because it follows a rib of rock and is relatively safe from rockfall. It is seldom climbed today because near the top the rock changes to loosely cemented cinder. **FA:** Gary Leech, Sept. 2, 1933 (Leech 1933).

Variation 1F: East Crater Wall. East Crater Wall may be the easiest and safest way to gain the top of the east crater rim. It begins due east of Crater Rock and follows a large cone of debris into a gully. At the top of Steel Cliff, follow Wy'east to the top. Like all steep faces on Mt. Hood, avoid this route unless it is well covered by snow and ice. **FA:** unknown.

2 Wy'east

Wy'east is a very popular route which gains the top of Steel Cliff and follows it to the summit. Although it can be done in summer conditions, the rotten rock near the top is best climbed in early season when it is covered with snow.

From the east side of Timberline Lodge, hike up to Silcox Hut. From Silcox Hut choose one of two approaches. If it is early in the climbing season, head toward Steel Cliff and cross White River Glacier at about 9,400 feet. If it is late in the season, cut east from Silcox Hut and cross lower White River Glacier. Gain the east lateral moraine and follow it to the south end of Steel Cliff.

Do not climb Steel Cliff directly. Circle right to the Newton Clark Glacier side of the ridge, then up the east side of the ridge to the top. The angle of the east side is about 35 to 40 degrees. It can be one of the more hazardous avalanche slopes on the mountain. Follow the rim of Steel Cliff to the crumbling rock walls of the main summit. Traverse east and up into a snow couloir. The couloir is steep, about 50 degrees, and leads directly to the summit. Time from Timberline Lodge, 6-10 hours.

Variation 2A. There is one major variation on Wy'east worth recording. The climb threads its way through several rock chimneys on the south side of Steel Cliff and gains the rim of Steel Cliff more directly and more quickly.

Mt. Hood from the East

Don Lowe photo

From the east lateral moraine of White River Glacier, proceed up the south face of Steel Cliff. Instead of circling right toward Newton Clark Glacier, climb up to and through a break in the cliff. Diagonal up and left on a 40-to 45-degree ramp to the top of Steel Cliff, and rejoin the regular route. The variation was originally done as a rock climb, but is more enjoyable when covered with snow or ice.

FRA: O.D. Miller J.W. Blakeney, C.C. Grimes, E.B. McFarland, and O.D. Doane, July 30, 1872 (Doane 1872). Historically, Wy'east is an important route on Mt. Hood. James Mount and Everett Darr named it in 1932 in honor of a small organization of mountaineers called the Wy'east Climbers (Darr 1932; Mount 1932). Darr and Mount thought they were doing a first ascent, and were baffled to find a fixed rope in the 50-degree couloir near the top. This rope was probably left over from the 1890s, when guides from Cloud Cap Inn sometimes used the Southeast Ridge as an alternative to Cooper Spur. Will Langille led the first guided ascent on Sept. 19, 1890. His clients were A.B. McAlpin and Lewis H. Adams. Langille named it the Finger Route after a prominent rock spire on the ridge, then called the Finger. Like Darr and Mount, Langille also thought that his climb was a first ascent (H; Langille 1937).

The confusion does not end there. Before the 1872 climb, there were at least three attempts to climb Wy'east. The first and most famous attempt was by T.J. Dryer in 1854. Dryer was owner and publisher of the *Oregonian*. In his newspaper he described his climb of Wy'east and claimed to be the first to reach the top of Mt. Hood. Because his description of the last part of the route was vague, members of a party that reached the summit in 1857, and many subsequent historians, questioned whether Dryer had ever been near the summit (Dierdorff 1857). Dryer's personality probably contributed to the controversy as much as his vague description. He was outspoken on the issues of the day and wrote bombastic editorials and personal attacks in the *Oregonian*.

FRA of Variation 2A: Everett Darr and James Mount, Aug. 7, 1932. Unpublished manuscripts by both men state that they climbed the eastern moraine of White River Glacier, and climbed the low-angle rock on the south-facing buttress that forms the end of Steel Cliff.

3 Newton Clark Headwall

Newton Clark Headwall bypasses Steel Cliff and climbs the steep slopes directly above Newton Clark Glacier to the final 300 feet of Wy'east. Climb early in the season to avoid rockfall. The Headwall is not a very popular route.

FA: unknown. Recent guidebooks attribute the first ascent of this route to Will and Doug Langille. Will Langille, in a letter to Fred McNeil, states that he never climbed this route (Langille 1937).

4 Cooper Spur

The advantages of climbing Cooper Spur are its easy approach from Cloud Cap Inn and direct line to the summit. The disadvantages of Cooper Spur are that the final 2,000 feet are dangerously exposed and tiring. It can be used as a descent route for north side climbs, but many parties arrange for a car shuttle and descend the South Side. Do not descend Cooper Spur during heavy snowfall, as avalanche danger is high, or during periods of hot weather, as the snow becomes excessively soft from day-long exposure to direct sun. If you decide to descend Cooper Spur, stay alert. Countless parties have fallen from the upper slopes; in fact, one rescue volunteer states that Cooper Spur is a popular route to fall off of. The resulting slide down the fall line is a perilous journey to the upper Eliot Glacier and has killed at least 10 people.

Start at Cloud Cap Saddle Campground. Follow Timberline Trail (USFS 600), south one mile to the east Eliot Glacier moraine. Leave Timberline Trail and follow a climbers' trail up to the top of Cooper Spur and past an obvious boulder called Tie-in-Rock. Climb a 45-degree, 2,000-foot snow slope through several rock bands to the summit. The final pitch to the top is close to 50 degrees. Time from Cloud Cap Saddle, 6-8 hours.

FA: Will and Doug Langille, August 21, 1891 (Grauer 1975). Fastest time from Cloud Cap, 1 hour 57 minutes, George Riddell, 1912 (Biewener 1956).

5 North Face

Traditionally this route has been called the North Face. This can be confusing because the climb actually follows the northeast face of the mountain. Call it what you will, the line is one of the best on Mt. Hood when the weather is cold and the snow is consolidated and icy.

Running up the middle of the northeast face of Mt. Hood is a rock rib, flanked on either side by shallow couloirs. The most commonly climbed route follows the right couloir. Avoid the Face when the freezing level is high or later in the season (usually after May), unless you enjoy a steady barrage of rockfall.

Approach from Cloud Cap Inn and lower Cooper Spur. Drop down on the Eliot glacier. Negotiate the bergschrund. This is sometimes the most difficult part of the climb. Move up to the base of the rock rib and follow the right-hand couloir (60 degrees) to a rock band. The rock band is about 40 feet long and about 65 degrees. If there is not enough ice on the rock, climb around it on the left or right. Above the first rock band, climb a 55-degree couloir to a second rock band. Climb it directly if there is enough ice. Pass it on the left if it is bare. After the second rock band, move right behind Cathedral Spire and continue up to the summit, or traverse left to Cooper Spur. Time from Cloud Cap Saddle, 6-10 hours.

Variation 5A. Early ascents of the Face followed the rock rib. It is technically easy (fourth-class), but the rock is rotten and unnerving.

Variation 5B. Climb a couloir to the left of the rock rib. The left couloir is not quite as steep as the right couloir. More than halfway up the couloir, pass the rock band on the right if there is not enough ice.

FRA: Mark Weygandt, Arthur Emmons, and Orville Emmons, August 26, 1928 (H; *Hood River News* 1928). Mark Weygandt stated that the Northeast Face was climbed in 1902. Mark did not give the climbers' names, nor could the climb be found in the early summit registers.

Colin Chisholm and James McRae completed the second ascent of this route in July or August of 1930 (Chisholm 1981). Russ McJury and Bill Hackett

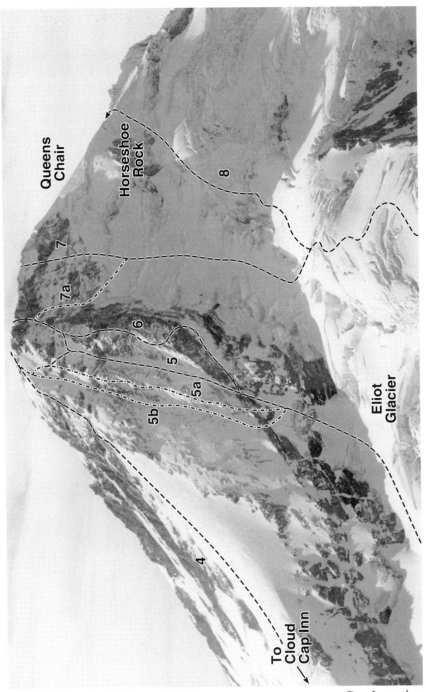

Mt. Hood from the North.   *Don Lowe photo*

completed the third ascent on June 28, 1936 (McJury 1936). The 1936 climb differed significantly from the 1928 and 1930 climbs. Once they reached the top of the rib, the first two parties escaped up and left onto the top portions of Cooper Spur. During separate interviews in 1981, both McJury and Hackett confirmed that they moved up and right onto the North Face Cleaver and finished up that route to the summit.

Dave Bohn, Art Maki, and Al Combs, climbed the North Face on May 19, 1958 via the right couloir without rock climbing on either side (Combs 1985; H).

6 North Face Cleaver

The North Face Cleaver is a prominent rock buttress which splits the north side of Mt. Hood. The Cleaver culminates 500 feet from the summit in the form of Cathedral Spire. Despite the beautiful line, the rock on the lower Cleaver is dangerous. One climber described it as "slimy sludge." Another climber said the rock, "looked like it was squeezed out of a giant toothpaste tube."

The first ascent party stayed on the rock, if that is what it can be called, and climbed the buttress directly. Most climbers avoid the bottom of the buttress, climb up the couloir on the left, and traverse right onto the easier upper section of the Cleaver. Either way, the route is not recommended.

FRA: Allen Steck and Dick Long, June 1961 (Steck 1985).

7 Eliot Glacier Headwall

Eliot Glacier Headwall is a large cirque to the right of The North Face Cleaver. Above the Eliot Glacier bergschrund, it is probably the steepest and most difficult headwall on Mt. Hood, averaging somewhere between 50 and 65 degrees, with occasionally steeper bulges. Do not attempt this route unless you have some rock climbing experience. There is a steep cliff near the top of the headwall which often is not bridged by snow or ice. Avoid this route after May unless the freezing level is low and the winter snowpack is high. Eliot Glacier Headwall has been climbed in October. The face is in the shade all day at this time of year, and in the right conditions, 1,000 feet of water ice will form.

Begin at Cloud Cap Saddle Campground. Follow the Sunshine Route to the top of the Snow Dome. Climb up to the bergschrund. Cross the bergschrund and climb the face slightly right of center. Near the summit, climb over a short rock cliff. Take ice screws and rock protection. Time from Cloud Cap, 8-12 hours.

Variation 7A. Stay close to the North Face Cleaver. Gain the col behind Cathedral Spire and follow the last 500 feet of the North Face.

FA: Russ McJury and Joe Leuthold, July 10, 1938 (H).

FA 7A: Dave Bohn, Art Maki, and Al Combs May 18, 1958 (Combs 1985).

8 Sunshine

The route is called Sunshine because it receives sunlight all day. It is an excellent line, primarily because it follows snow-and-ice, and you never have to climb rock. Sunshine is longer than Cooper Spur, Wy'east, or the South Side, and requires more experience in route finding, snow and ice climbing, and safe glacier travel.

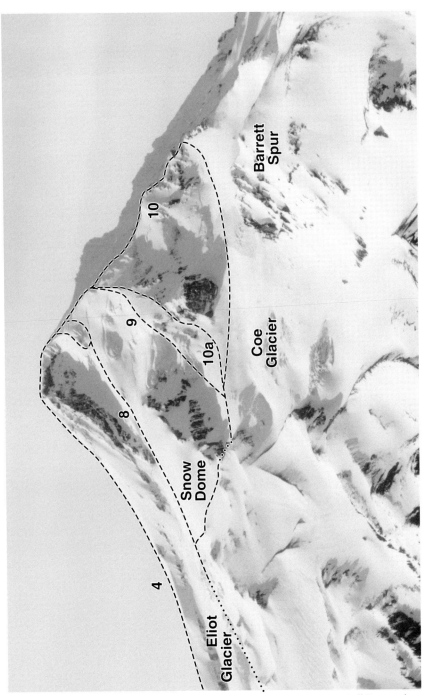

Mt. Hood from the North

Bill Bryan photo

Start at Cloud Cap Saddle Campground. Follow Timberline Trail (USFS 600) south one mile to the east Eliot Glacier moraine. Leave Timberline Trail and follow a climbers' trail up Cooper Spur. Near the top of Cooper Spur, drop down the moraine and onto Eliot glacier using a rough but obvious trail. Cross Eliot Glacier between the upper and lower icefalls, and gain a rounded and less broken-up section called the Snow Dome.

The Snow Dome can also be reached by hiking west along Timberline Trail (USFS 600), toward Elk Cove. After about six minutes of hiking, cross Eliot Creek and follow switchbacks up a steep hill. At the top of the hill, the trail rounds a short bend and crosses a very small meadow. Leave the main trail and follow a climbers' trail up through the meadow and into the woods. Move left to the crest of the west lateral moraine of Eliot Glacier, and follow the moraine for about an hour to where it joins the upper reaches of Langille Crags at a short 50-foot cliff. Skirt the cliff on the right and continue up broad slopes to The Snow Dome.

Move up the Snow Dome to Anderson Rock. Climb steeper slopes up to the bergschrund beneath Horseshoe Rock. The bergschrund, especially later in the season, can be difficult. If you can, pass it to the right of Horseshoe Rock. If this is not possible pass the bergschrund to the left of Horseshoe Rock. Above the bergschrund, climb up and right to Cathedral Ridge, then follow the ridge up and left to the summit. Time from Cloud Cap Saddle, 9-11 hours.

Sunshine is climbed year-round, however the difficulty increases in late summer and early fall. Without snow cover, the upper reaches of Cathedral Ridge are unenjoyable scree fields. The best time to climb Sunshine is during May or June except in years of unusually high snowfall.

FA: Will Langille and G.W. Graham, Sept. 3, 1892 (Grauer 1975).

9 Coe Glacier Icefall

If you want technical ice climbing, try Coe Glacier Icefall in Sept. and Oct. when the freezing level is down. It is not a route for beginners and often turns back very experienced parties. Enter the icefall prepared to climb steep if not vertical glacier ice. Hardhats are a must because of rockfall. Most climbing parties stop at the top of the Icefall and return to Cloud Cap.

Start at Cloud Cap and follow Sunshine. Once you are on Snow Dome descend to Coe Glacier. In late summer, descending to Coe Glacier can be tricky because of poor rock. Climb through the icefall. Follow Sunshine or Cathedral Ridge to the summit, or walk back down Snow Dome and return to Cloud Cap.

FRA: Jim Lill and Wendell Stout, September 12, 1937 (H).

10 Cathedral Ridge

Cathedral Ridge is not technically difficult, but it is difficult to reach. Climb Cathedral Ridge when is is covered by snow. Without snow, you must slog up loose scree which yields one foot down for every two feet up.

From Timberline Lodge, approach via Illumination Saddle, Reid Glacier, and Sandy Glacier. Once on Sandy Glacier, traverse to a gully on lower Cathedral Ridge, or if snow conditions allow, use Variation 10C.

From Cloud Cap, climb to the base of Pulpit Rock. Continue west past Pulpit Rock and Ladd Glacier cirque. Climb up the spur on the west side of Ladd Glacier. Once on the ridge traverse around the left side of a large gendarme. Several hundred feet higher, pass another larger gendarme, again on its left side. Continue on the west side of the ridge to the top of the Queens Chair and on to the summit. Time from Timberline Lodge or Cloud Cap Saddle, at least 11 hours.

From McNeil Point Shelter, follow gentle slopes up to Cathedral Ridge at approximately 6,800 feet. Drop slightly to the north toward Glisan Glacier to avoid a series of rock spires on the crest of Cathedral Ridge. Rejoin the Ridge at about 8,200 feet and follow it to where a spur between Ladd and Glisan Glaciers joins at about 9,100 feet. Pass two gendarmes on the left, and continue on easier ground to the Queens Chair and the summit.

Variation 10A: Pulpit Rock. Climb the east side of Pulpit Rock. Gain Cathedral Ridge and follow it to the summit. Not recommended.

Variation 10B: Ladd Headwall. Ladd Headwall is a variation on Cathedral Ridge for parties coming from Cloud Cap Inn. Climb before June when the Ladd bergschrund usually forms an impassable moat (Pooley 1976).

Variation 10C: Use 10C in early season when approaching from Illumination Rock to avoid lower Cathedral Ridge.

FA: Newton Clark, William J. Smith, and J. Elmer Rand, August 11, 1887 (H). The summit register entry is August 10, 1887, but the date is changed later in a newspaper account to August 11, 1887 (Oregonian 1887).

FRA of Pulpit Rock: Irving B. Lincoln, June 28, 1936 (Darr 1937). Wesley Weygandt states that his father, Mark Weygandt, climbed Pulpit Rock long before 1936. However likely this may be, Wesley's assertion could not be confirmed.

FRA of Ladd Headwall: Dick Pooley, Charlie Martin, Jim Davis, Bud Seigel, and Brian Hukari, May 16, 1976.

11 Sandy Glacier Headwall

Sandy Glacier Headwall takes a direct line up the west face of Mt. Hood. Though it is highly visible from Portland, the Headwall is isolated and not commonly climbed because of its distance from convenient access.

The steep section of Sandy Glacier Headwall is slightly longer than Leuthold Couloir or Reid Glacier Headwall, but the average angle is about the same. You must climb this route early in the season to minimize rockfall hazard.

Hike to Illumination Saddle. Drop down and cross the Reid Glacier. Traverse around Yocum Ridge at 8,600 feet and descend to the Sandy Glacier. You must not attempt to cross Yocum Ridge in the dark unless you are familiar with the route. The traverse is not obvious and the ground is steep in several places.

Traverse north across Sandy Glalcier. Start up the Headwall. Follow moderate slopes (45 degrees) through a narrow hourglass and continue up to the Queens Chair. Continue on to the summit. (Remember to traverse the Sandy Glacier a fair distance before starting up the Headwall. If you start too soon, you will end up below the steep walls of the Upper Buttrees of Yocum Ridge. Even in the best conditions this Buttress is difficult to climb.)

Mt. Hood from the Northwest   *Leonard Delano photo*

Sandy Glacier Headwall can also be approached from McNeil Point.

FA: Joe Leuthold and Russ McJury, June 6, 1937 (H). Their line of ascent was several hundred feet to the right of what is today considered the easiest route. Their route has been repeated several times but only under winter conditions (McNeil *Journal* 1937; Monner 1938).

The first known ascent of the easier route was by Fred Ayres, Keith Petrie, Dave Hitchcock, and Don McKay on May 19, 1956 (Hitchcock 1988).

12 Yocum Ridge

Yocum Ridge, with or without the **First Gendarme Variation**, is one of the most spectacular and sought-after climbs in the Pacific Northwest. Despite this, very few parties complete the entire route. Rotten rock towers guard its crest. They cannot be climbed unless they are covered with a thick layer of rime ice. Contrary to what common sense would dictate, rime ice is more solid than the rock on Yocum Ridge. The catch is that rime ice is often impossible to protect. Take your ice tools, pickets, and other technology, but know that on this route the old advice still holds true; the leader must not fall.

Hike from Timberline Lodge to Illumination Saddle. Drop down and cross Reid Glacier, and gain Yocum Ridge at about 8,600 feet. Follow the Ridge to the First Gendarme, a large rock tower which appears to block all access.

From Fred Beckey's description in the 1960 American Alpine Journal, it is obvious that this obstacle was passed on the right during the original climb, and that Beckey and Scheiblehner soon regained the ridge crest.

> *A mushrooming tower threatened progress and so Leo decided to try the south flank. After chopping downward and across a groove, he disappeared around a hidden corner. Some 15 minutes later he came into view again, cutting up a gully-wall that needed both hand and footholds.*

Today, most parties traverse lower and longer than the first ascent party, skirting the First and Second Gendarme on steep ramps roughly 600 feet horizontally along the south flank of the Ridge. The ramps quit, forcing the route up steep gullies and chimneys to the Third Gendarme. Climb the ridge crest of the Third Gendarme. The Gendarme ends at an obvious drop-off next to a short rock pillar. Sling the pillar and rappel. The rock pillar looks unstable, and probably is. Take lots of sling, and rappel carefully.

Two different ways have been found to complete the rappel. The first ascent party rappelled to the ridge and followed the crest to the base of the upper buttress. This is apparently not too bad as long as there is a good layer of snow cementing things together. Alternatively, some parties have bypassed the crest of the ridge and rappelled a full 150 feet to a 60-to 65-degree slope on the north side. Traverse the slope under the ridge (the angle quickly eases to about 45 degrees) and regain the crest. Follow it to the base of the upper buttress (excellent bivy site). Either method may be preferable on a given day, depending on the condition of the rime ice.

Mt. Hood from the West   *Terry Toedtemeier photo*

Yocum Ridge   *Philip N. Jones photo*

The route from the base of the buttress up to the Queens Chair seems to be the same today as when Beckey and Scheiblehner climbed it in 1959. Move right and descend one-half rope-length down a gully on the south side. This gully can also be used to escape the Ridge by descending into Leuthold Couloir (see variations). Traverse up and right along a snow gully several pitches to a couloir. Follow the couloir to the top of the buttress. Follow the ridge to the Queens Chair. Climb to the summit or descend Leuthold Couloir and return to Illumination Saddle.

The first ascent party completed Yocum Ridge in one long day. Many parties have been forced to bivouac or downclimb the gully leading to Leuthold Couloir and return another day.

Variation 12A: First Gendarme. An even more difficult and spectacular line is to tackle the First Gendarme. According to a member of the first ascent-party, the First Gendarme is:

> *near-vertical for approximately 15 feet, about 100 feet to 120 feet lead overall. Too bad the frightful part is near the top. Huge (3 to 4 foot) pickets offer the best hope of protection? Flukes would be useless, as would screws.* (Young 1984)

Variation 12B: Retreat Gully. The Retreat Gully is about 50 degrees. It leads from Leuthold Couloir to the base of the upper buttress on Yocum Ridge. The gully is the safest and easiest way to get off Yocum Ridge.

Variation 12C: Sandy Headwall Traverse. From the base of the upper buttress on Yocum Ridge, it is possible to traverse left (north) to the upper slopes of Sandy Glacier Headwall.

Variation 12D: Sandy Headwall Gully. This gully leads from the Sandy Glacier to the base of the upper buttress of Yocum Ridge. It is an excellent climb if snow conditions are good. The steepest section of the couloir is about 65 degrees.

FA: Fred Beckey and Leo Scheiblehner, April 10, 1959.

FA via First Gendarme: Del Young and Terry Hiatt, March 1, 1972.

FA of other variations: unknown.

13 Leuthold Couloir

Leuthold Couloir is a deservedly popular climb. It is more accessible than Sandy Glacier Headwall and the average angle of the route is a moderate 40 to 45 degrees. Climb Leuthold Couloir in early season to avoid heavy rockfall. Avoid the gully during and immediately after a storm because of avalanche danger.

Climb the south side to Illumination Saddle. Descend about 150 feet to the head of Reid Glacier. Normally this descent is easy, but the angle fluctuates with the amount of drifting snow, and the upper half of the slope can be very steep. Contour north past a low buttress of rock to the base of a large couloir paralleling the south flank of Yocum Ridge. Follow the couloir through a narrow opening called the Hourglass, and continue up to the Queens Chair and the summit.

FA: Jim Mount and Ralph Calkin, Sept. 4, 1932 (Mount 1932). The original name of Leuthold Couloir was Yocum Ridge Route. To avoid confusing the route

Mt. Hood from the West   *Don Lowe photo*

with Yocum Ridge, Everett Darr renamed the climb Avalanche Route in 1936. Subsequent names have included the West Face or the Hourglass. The current name honors the memory of one of Oregon's finest climbers, Joe Leuthold.

14 Reid Glacier Headwall

There are several ways to climb Reid Glacier Headwall. The longest and most interesting way follows two narrow gullies and ends at Queens Chair. The average angle of this line is 40-to 45-degrees, with perhaps one 50-degree bulge.

Climb the South Side to Illumination Saddle. Descend 150 feet from Illumination Saddle to the Reid Glacier. Normally this descent is easy, but the angle can fluctuate and the upper half of the slope can be very steep. Contour around the head of Reid Glacier toward Leuthold Couloir. Halfway across the headwall, climb straight up into a narrow canyon. Emerging from the canyon, climb left onto a rib of snow then climb into a second, narrower canyon. Emerging from the second canyon, climb up and left to a viewpoint overlooking Leuthold Couloir and the upper buttress on Yocum Ridge. Climb up to the summit ridge.

Variations 14A & 14B. Several gullies lead from Reid Glacier to Castle Crags and west crater rim. See the photos for details.

FRA: Gordon Facer, Marshall Cronyn, and R.J. (Joe) Corruccini, June 12, 1938. Facer, Cronyn, and Corruccini were three Reed College students who got lost on the Reid Glacier in a fog bank trying to find Leuthold Couloir. Turning up too soon, they managed to climb the Headwall. When contacted nearly 50 years later, not only could all three remember the climb, but all three were able to furnish contemporary written accounts (H; Corruccini 1986).

FA of variations: unknown. According to an unpublished manuscript written by Gary Leech in the 1930s, the gullies leading from Reid Glacier to the rim above Castle Crags were climbed before 1933.

15 Castle Crags

Castle Crags is a mammoth rock buttress, crowned with savage rock towers. It begins above Illumination Saddle at roughly 9,400 feet and ends at approximately 10,200 feet where it loses its incredible topography and mellows into the pleasant ridge called the West Crater Rim. Climbing the crest of the Crags is easier in late spring conditions when more rock is exposed than it is in winter when rime ice covers the rock. Some climbers claim that in full rime ice conditions, Castle Crags is harder than Yocum Ridge.

From Illumination Saddle, proceed up snow slopes below the crags. Follow snow ramps up and left around a prominent buttress which forms the beginning of the Crags. Above, either follow a couloir or a snow shoulder up to a notch in the ridge. Climb the ridge, skirting or climbing over rock towers. When the ridge merges with the west crater rim, descend Zigzag Glacier or climb to the summit.

Variation 15A. Instead of gaining the crest and climbing over the towers, traverse the headwall under the towers.

FA: Gary Leech, Sept. 13, 1933. Leech approached the spires from above by climbing out the ridge, toward the south (Leech 1933). The route as described in this book, coming up from Illumination Saddle, was climbed July 7, 1951 by Russ McJury, Dave Wagstaff, and Dave Young (Wagstaff 1985).

ILLUMINATION ROCK (Approximately 9500')

A few more rods placed me on the overhanging summit monolith (which I predict will fall within ten years).
Gary Leech, commenting on the summit of Illumination Rock in 1936

Illumination Rock is a well-known and spectacular landmark on the southwest side of Mt. Hood. Because of glacial action, there are only three sides to the Rock, north, south, and southeast, and its current shape roughly resembles a fish fin oriented on an east-west axis.

There are three summits along the crest of the rock; the west, the middle, and the east. The eastern summit, a huge overhanging block, is the highest.

The volcanic rock of Illumination Rock is good when compared to the rest of Mt. Hood, but is terrible when contrasted to what modern rock climbers prefer. Still, to paraphrase Tom Patey, any fool can climb good rock; it takes a special fool to climb bad rock.

West Arete (II-5.1)

The greatest difficulty with this route is dealing with the rotten rock. Approach the West Arete from Zigzag Glacier. Follow a gully on the southwest end of Illumination Rock to the top of the west ridge. In the summer the gully is filled with scree. Follow fourth-or easy fifth-class rock up the ridge to a small subsidiary summit called the West Gable. Skirt the West Gable on the left and continue up fourth-class rock to the summit rim. Follow the rim 300 feet to the overhanging summit block on the east end. To descend, return to the West Gable and rappel from a large boulder which is usually festooned with slings.

FA: Ray Conway, 1913 (Leech 1954).

South Wall (easy fifth-class)

A prominent feature of the south face of Illumination Rock is a large natural amphitheater called the South Chamber. Climb the lower West Arete, and traverse from the arete onto the buttress on the left side of the Chamber. Climb the buttress to a gendarme below the west summit called the West Gable. Continue up the West Arete to the summit crest. Follow the crest 300 feet to the overhanging summit block on the east end. To descend, return to the West Gable and rappel from a large boulder which is usually festooned with slings. Not recommended.

FA: Gary Leech, July 1, 1936 (Ill).

South Chamber Route (II-5.4)

Begin on the Zigzag Glacier. Climb into the South Chamber, an upside-down tear-shaped scree bowl. In summer, a short 15-to 20-foot wall will have to be climbed to gain the bottom of the Chamber. Climb up to the top of the Chamber.

Face climb left over blocks (5.4) until you are under the West Gable. Climb straight up to the Gable and continue up the West Arete. Follow the summit ridge 300 feet to the overhanging summit block on the east end. Take a small rock rack of 10 to 15 pieces. To descend, return to the West Gable and rappel down the West Arete from a large boulder which is usually festooned with slings.

FA: Smoke Blanchard, 1945 (Dodge 1965).

South Face (II-5.1)

Climb into the South Chamber. Wander up and right over steep but broken slabs to the overhanging summit block. Descend via the West Arete.

Northeast Face (II-5.8)

Huge freight-car-sized rocks peeled off this face in 1939 and 1957 (and probably at other times unnoticed or unrecorded). Two routes were erased, the original 1933 East Arete route by Gary Leech, and the Keyhole, developed by Gary Leech and Smoke Blanchard in 1938. Unknown climbers developed the following line sometime after 1957. The rock is dangerously loose. Avoid this route unless you need to descend from the summit quickly.

From Illumination Saddle follow the east ridge of Illumination Rock over many large unstable looking boulders. Move right 10 feet at the base of the main cliff, and climb up 30 feet to a 3/8" bolt. Traverse right 20 feet to the base of a short headwall with cracks on the right and left. Climb the right-hand crack. Continue up to the crest of ridge just below the summit and cross over to the south face of Illumination Rock. Traverse west past the summit block and climb it from the west. Descend off a slinged block just east of the summit. Two ropes will reach easy ground, one rope will force a second rappel off the 3/8" bolt.

North Face (II-5.5)

From Illumination Saddle follow the east ridge of Illumination Rock over many large, unstable-looking boulders. From the base of the main cliff, drop slightly and follow an easy ledge onto the north face. Continue to traverse west across the north face until an obvious system of ledges and cracks leads upward. Climb straight up. Near the top, climb a hand-and-fist crack straight up to a natural skylight in the summit ridge. Move east and climb the overhanging summit block. Descend to Illumination Saddle or down the West Arete. Rotten rock, not recommended.

FA via a slightly different finish: Gary Leech and Smoke Blanchard, August 20, 1938 (Leech 1933).

Climbers on the summit pinnacle of Illumination Rock.   *Dave Hitchcock photo*

West Side traverse under The Pinnacle from Red Saddle   *Don Alan Hall photo*

MT. JEFFERSON (10,497')

Mr. Looney, in company with myself, ascended the peak on the south; this we found no difficulty in doing....There is however, one rock standing on, and which finishes the peak, which no man can possibly ascend, rising in height 100 feet, and forming an impassable barrier to the adventurer.

E.L. Massey 1854

DESCRIPTION

Mount Jefferson is the second highest mountain in Oregon, with an official altitude of 10,497 feet. It has a reputation as the most difficult summit in the Oregon Cascades because you must climb a 400 foot pinnacle to reach the highest point. Many climbers fail to climb The Pinnacle. Rime ice coats the steep rock walls eight to nine months out of the year, and an exposed traverse on snow or ice guards access to the easiest route. Even if you have climbed The Pinnacle, it still looks formidable on subsequent attempts.

The north side of Mt. Jefferson is one of the wildest alpine settings in Oregon. Three ridges descend from the summit rim. Between the ridges are two glaciers, the Jefferson Park Glacier on the left and the Russell Glacier on the right. Above the glaciers, the rim is a series of rock cliffs and towers. The most prominent towers are the Mohler Tooth on the left and Smith Rock on the right. Further west of Smith Rock, and visible only from certain vantage points, is a minor but important formation called Prehistoric Monster. Mohler Tooth and Smith Rock are not official names. They are used to clarify route descriptions and to honor Sidney S. Mohler of Oregon City and David B. Smith of Gates, Oregon, the first two individuals to climb Mt. Jefferson from the north. Below the towers, ridges, and glaciers, at an approximate altitude of 5,800 feet is a broad flat valley originally known as Hanging Valley, but now known as Jefferson Park. Two more glaciers can be found on Mt. Jefferson, Whitewater on the east side and Waldo, a small pocket glacier, on the southeast side. In 1907 the Milk Creek Cirque on the west side contained a large glacier (Hatch 1917). According to the Oregon Statesman, part or all of this Glacier was destroyed when it slid 500 feet down Milk Creek in July of 1977.

The best time to climb Mount Jefferson from the north, east, or west is in late spring when snow is plentiful and rockfall less likely. Climbers use The Southwest Ridge and South Ridge throughout the year because neither route is vulnerable to rockfall. Winter climbs are rare. The approach involves one to two days of hard skiing. Those who succeed in reaching the summit in winter earn the privilege.

MAPS

The following maps are currently (1991) available for Mt. Jefferson.
1. Mount Jefferson, 7.5 minute quadrangle, published by USGS in 1988.
2. Mount Jefferson Wilderness, published by the USFS in 1979.
3. Mount Jefferson Recreation Map, published 1984 by Geo-Graphics of Portland, Oregon. Revised edition due in 1991.

ROADS AND TRAILS

Driving through the Warm Springs Indian Reservation to a trailhead on the east side of Mt. Jefferson is absolutely prohibited by the Tribal Council. There are no exceptions, and the policy is enforced. Approaches to the mountain are therefore limited to west side USFS roads branching off State Highway 22.

Whitewater Road (USFS 2243), Whitewater Trail, and Pacific Crest Trail.

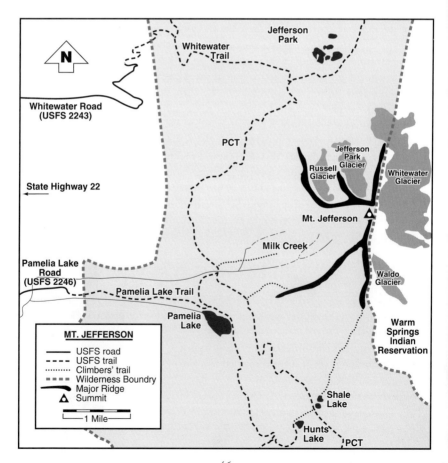

This route provides the best access to Jefferson Park. Most parties camp in Jefferson Park or bivy above the Park at extreme timberline. Three trails lead to Jefferson Park, including the South Breitenbush Trail and the PCT from the north, but the Whitewater Trail is the shortest and easiest.

Drive 10 miles east of Detroit on State Highway 22. Turn east on Whitewater Road, USFS 2243. Drive about 7.5 miles to the road's end. Follow Whitewater Trail north up the hill about 1.5 miles. At a junction with a second trail, turn right (south) and hike about 2.5 miles to the PCT. Turn left (north) and follow the PCT less than a mile into Jefferson Park.

Pamelia Lake Road (USFS 2246), Pamelia Lake Trail, and Hunts Lake or Shale Lake. This route provides the best approach to the southwest and south sides of the mountain. Good campsites exist at Pamelia Lake, but its low elevation severely penalizes any party trying to reach Mt. Jefferson's summit. A camp at Hunts Lake or Shale Lake, or a timberline bivouac above the PCT, will put climbing parties in a better position for the following day's climb.

Drive 12 miles east of Detroit on State Highway 22. One-quarter mile north of Pamelia Creek, turn left (east) on Pamelia Lake Road (USFS 2246) and drive about four miles to road's end.

Hike east about 2.3 miles to a signposted intersection on the northwest end of Pamelia Lake. Continue left uphill toward the PCT. Hike less than five minutes to a second intersection. Turn left to approach the Southwest Ridge and the PCT. Turn right to reach Hunts Lake. Shale Lake can be reached from either direction. Shale Lake via the PCT is less direct and longer (seven miles), but the route follows a good trail at an easy gradient. Shale Lake via Hunts Lake is shorter, but the climbers' trail from Hunts Lake is unimproved and steep.

Winter Access. Whitewater Road leaves Highway 22 at about 2,180 feet above sea level. Pamelia Lake Road leaves Highway 22 at about 2,300 feet. Because both roads start so low, the distance to Mt. Jefferson in winter can fluctuate considerably, depending on snowline.

In winter, do not take Whitewater Trail. You will find it faster and easier to leave the Whitewater Road at the large hairpin curve at 3,600 feet, and continue east up Whitewater Creek.

USFS SPECIAL AREA REGULATIONS

Besides general regulations which apply to all USFS wilderness areas in Oregon (see Introduction), the following specific areas have additional restrictions.

1. **Jefferson Park Area Restrictions.** No camping on Scout Lake Peninsula and Bays Lake Peninsula.
2. **Marion Lake Area Restrictions.** No overnight camping. No building, maintaining, attending, or using a fire, campfire, or stovefire. No Grazing or tethering livestock for more than four hours. No storing equipment, personal property, or supplies for more than eight hours.

DESCENT

Most parties return to Jefferson Park by descending Whitewater Glacier. If you bivy above Jefferson Park and climb a north-side route, you will save time by descending diagonally down North Milk Creek Cirque to the ridge above the head of Russell Glacier. Descend to Russell Glacier and follow it north. Cut east below the snout of Jefferson Park Glacier. Slog up an old lateral moraine and follow it down to your camp. Do not use this descent if the snow has melted out of upper Milk Creek Cirque. In an emergency, descend the Southwest Ridge to the PCT.

ROUTES UP THE PINNACLE

The Pinnacle has two summits, the north horn and the south horn. The north horn is slightly higher. No matter what the conditions–dry rock, verglas, or full armor of rime ice–the best way to reach either summit is to climb the west face of the north horn. This face is easily gained from the north because the north ridge leading to The Pinnacle is level and the slopes under the west face are low angle.

Gaining the west face of the north horn from the south can be difficult. From Red Saddle, work down slightly and traverse 200 to 250 feet of steep snow or ice under the rotten west face of the south horn. The traverse is unnerving because of the exposure below, and dangerous because of the possibility of rock and icefall from above.

The difficulty of the traverse eases once you gain a small shoulder. From the shoulder you can climb straight up on steep but relatively solid rock (5.1), or continue north and climb up a lower-angle fourth-class face. If The Pinnacle is coated with rime ice the climbing will be much more difficult.

The west gully between the northern and southern horns of The Pinnacle is filled with loose rock. Do not attempt this route unless all the rock is covered by snow. If the gully is covered with rime ice, the final 20 to 30 feet to the saddle between the horns can be a desperate struggle.

There are two or three attractive cracks on the upper southwest wall of the southern horn. The difficulty is about 5.6 or 5.7. Unfortunately, to get to the good stuff, you must survive the first hundred feet of junk. This rotten rock has calved off repeatedly in recent times, including one massive slide in 1951.

Climbing the east side of The Pinnacle is described in the route descriptions for Warm Springs Couloir, the East Arete and Whitewater Headwall.

ROUTES

1 Southwest Ridge

John Scott, a well known Mazama historian and climber, once said, "If I never climb this route again, it will be too soon." He was referring to the Southwest Ridge of Mt. Jefferson. The start at Pamelia Lake is too low (3,884 feet), and the

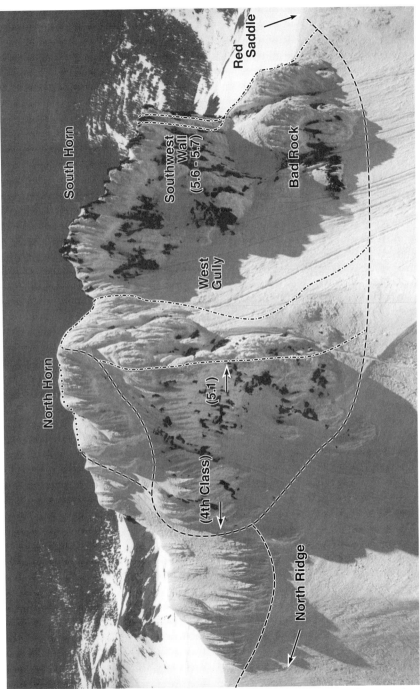

The Pinnacle of Mt. Jefferson from the West   *Terry Toedtemeier photo*

Waldo Glacier

Mt. Jefferson from the South

Leonard Delano photo

distance to the summit too long (nearly five miles). The Ridge is steep enough to be tiring, but not steep enough to be interesting. Once the snow melts, the absence of a good trail and abundance of scree and boulders insures that the trip down will be nearly as tedious as the trip up. During summer, take extra containers, as the only water available on the entire climb is just above Pamelia Lake.

To begin the climb, find an inconspicuous climbers' trail on the northeast side of Pamelia Lake which follows a seasonal stream up the hillside. Unless you have been down this trail it is very difficult to find from the bottom.

If you cannot find the climbers' trail, follow a short connector trail west and north from Pamelia Lake to its intersection with the PCT in Milk Creek Canyon. Turn right and follow the PCT south about 30 minutes. When the PCT passes through a manzanita-and-buckbrush clearing in a small canyon, turn uphill and follow a climbers' trail. When the trail enters the woods and the slope eases, move south onto the Southwest Ridge. If you lose the trail while still in the manzanita and buckbrush, do not try to thrash your way through the tangle. Turn around and try to get back on the trail, or move to the nearest trees and then move up.

Follow the Southwest Ridge, staying on or near its crest until joining the South Ridge near 9,800 feet. Above, move around and up the right side of a rock ridge and scramble up rocky-but-easy ground to the Red Saddle. Climb The Pinnacle. Time from Pamelia Lake, 7-12 hours. **FA:** unknown.

2 South Ridge

The one advantage of this monotonous line is that you will find camping and water within a reasonable distance to the summit. Camp at Hunts Lake (5,236 feet) in Hunts Cove, or Shale Lake (about 5,900 feet) along the Skyline Trail.

Attain Shale Lake from either Hunts Lake or the PCT. Shale Lake via the PCT is less direct and longer, seven miles from Pamelia Lake, but the route follows a good trail at an easy gradient. Shale Lake via Hunts Cove is shorter, but the climbers' trail out of Hunts Cove is unimproved and steep.

From Shale Lake, head northeast toward the South Ridge. Try to gain the ridge a bit north of Goat Peak. In early season it is much easier to follow any of the snow-filled gullies which converge higher up on the South Ridge.

Once on the South Ridge, follow the path of least resistance. Early summer climbers often find easier going on the snow slopes which persist to the east of the ridge line. Join the Southwest Ridge at approximately 9,800 feet. Above, move around and up the right side of a rock ridge and scramble up rocky-but-easy ground to the Red Saddle. Climb The Pinnacle. Time from Hunts Lake, 7-11 hours. Time from Shale Lake, 6-10 hours.

The descent to Shale Lake can be tricky. Once off the South Ridge, you will not be able to see your camp. If a storm or fogbank moves in, you will find it very easy to wander down the wrong gully. Some parties have spent hours locating their base. If the weather appears doubtful, consider marking the route on the way up. In good weather you will find excellent glissading when there is enough snow in the series of bowls just west of the ridge.

FA of South Ridge and The Pinnacle: Ray L. Farmer and E.C. Cross, Aug. 12,

1988 (Pearce 1900; *Mazama* 1907). E.L. Massey and Preston Looney climbed the South Ridge in 1854 (see quote at beginning of chapter). They and many subsequent parties gazed on The Pinnacle but did not attempt it. The first serious attempt to climb The Pinnacle was by Judge John Waldo and E.W. Bingham on Aug. 13, 1879. According to a note they left in an old whiskey bottle, Waldo and Bingham were within 100 feet of the summit, but could go no further (Newspaper unknown 1913).

3 Whitewater Glacier

Whitewater Glacier allows you to camp amidst the alpine beauty of Jefferson Park on the north side of the mountain, and climb up the easier slopes of the south side. Whitewater Glacier is also safe to travel in summer, and it gives the climber a grand tour of three sides of the mountain. The primary disadvantage of the route is its length--over 10 miles, round trip, from Russell Lake.

Most of the Whitewater Glacier is within the boundaries of the Warm Springs Indian Reservation. The tribal council asks that climbers write or call in advance for permission to cross their territory. A liaison has been set up with the USFS Ranger District in Detroit to facilitate this process. Since the tribe could ban climbing on the east side of Mt. Jefferson, you must follow this procedure.

Start by following a rocky climbers' trail up the right side of a stream which drains into Jefferson Park from Whitewater Glacier. Debris from a 1934 flood should be evident at the base of the stream. The trail climbs steeply, then flattens out briefly. Thread through a gap in the Whitewater Glacier moraines, and gain the glacier. Move south across the glacier, staying high to avoid crevasses lower down. Gain the Southeast Ridge and follow it to the Red Saddle at the base of The Pinnacle. Climb The Pinnacle. Time from Jefferson Park, 8-12 hours.

FRA: F.H. Jane and R. Nyden, Aug. 25, 1921 (J). This is undoubtedly not the first party to climb Whitewater Glacier, but they were the first to say so in the register. They actually climbed the South Ridge rather than the Southeast Ridge.

4 Warm Springs Couloir

Warm Springs Couloir is an obvious 50-to 55-degree gully which leads through the rock bands in the center of the east face of Mt. Jefferson. Approach from Jefferson Park. There are three cruxes on this climb: passing the bergschrund at the bottom, avoiding rockfall while in the couloir, and several pitches of fifth-class rock climbing on The Pinnacle. The first two cruxes are especially dependent on snow level and temperature. The first ascent party wrote of the lower gully, which is a natural funnel for rockfall, "In retrospect, we both found this maneuver (climbing the couloir) like playing Russian Roulette with a giant cannon."

FA: Nick Nicolai and T.C. Price Zimmermann, June 1969 (Nicolai 1969).

5 East Arete

The east arete is a hazardous climb. Phil Lizee, a member of the second ascent party, explains why.

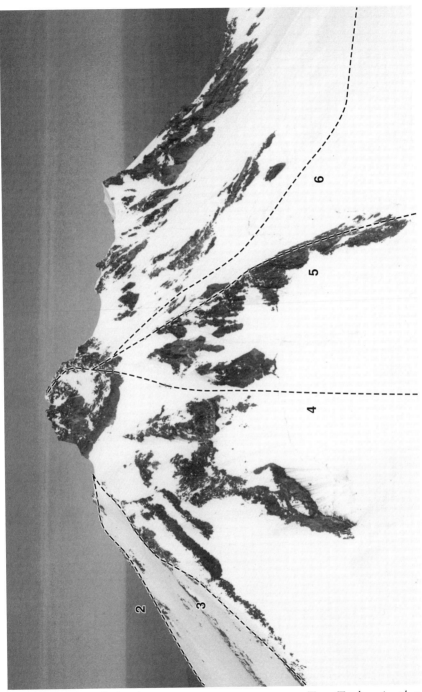

Mt. Jefferson from the South   *Terry Toedtemeier photo*

> *We climbed unroped on the cleaver only, because everything you
> touched or stepped on, was loose....the use of the rope, would have
> put the following climber in for too much danger from rockfall...I
> will freely admit that we lucked out, as we were nearly taken out
> twice by rockfall as we sweated our way upward; I mean big rocks,
> like wagon wheels, accompanied by smaller ones!* (Lizee 1984).

FA: Probably Armin Furrer and George Reuter, Sept. 4, 1932 (Scott 1933).

6 Whitewater Headwall

Whitewater Headwall climbs a steep face north of the East Arete and south of a
smaller rock rib, which for lack of a better term is called the East Spur. Pass two
bergschrunds at the bottom of the face and climb the headwall. At the top of the
face, gain a prominent rock rib, which is really an extension of the East Arete.
According to the first ascent party,

> *If the rock is gained on the north side of the rib it will probably
> be necessary to cross (as we did) to the south side for the final phase
> of the climb.*

The first ascent party described the rock as "loose" and the difficulty as "mostly
class 3 and 4." The second ascent party started rock climbing on the south side of
the rib and described the rock as "exceptionally solid." The second ascent party also
used the snowpatch, which starts halfway up The Pinnacle, to bypass several
pitches of rock climbing. Avoid this route after June.

FA: Peter Sheldrick and John Witte, July 5, 1964 (Sheldrick 1965).

7 East Spur

The East Spur is a forgettable rib of rock which ends short of the rim north of
The Pinnacle. Like the East Arete to the south, the East Spur is horrible rock.

FA: Peter Parsons, Aug. 26, 1924. Parsons' description is exact.

> *Left Jefferson Park at 6:00 a.m. arrived here at 9:45 a.m.
> followed around the mountain over the glacier on the east side, then
> up a rock spur to the saddle just north of this pinnacle which I also
> climbed from the North side.* (J)

8 East Face

The East Face is probably the easiest and safest route up the east side of Mt.
Jefferson, and has the added benefit of being the shortest route to The Pinnacle
from Jefferson Park. The word safest does not imply safe, especially in summer
conditions when the snow is soft and the temperature is high. Rockfall is a serious
problem, and slab and slush avalanches are not uncommon.

Start to the right of the East Spur, and pass the bergschrund. Climb the 45-

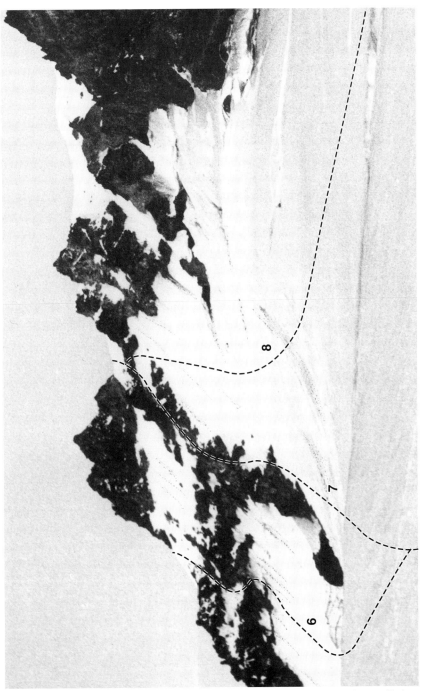

Mt. Jefferson from the Northeast   *Don Alan Hall photo*

degree snowfield above. Near the rock walls at the top, move left (south) to where the East Spur narrows. Cross the Spur and move up to the rim north of The Pinnacle. The final pitch to the top is probably 50 degrees, and in early season a cornice may block access to the rim.

FD: John Scott, Aug. 1925.

FA: Lynn Darcy, Paul Spangler, and Ed H. Marshall, August 8, 1933 (Scott 1933). For many years, the first ascent of this route was attributed to E.M. Pry and Harry Wolfe on August 22, 1922. The correct name of the first climber is E. Morgan Pryse. Evidence provided by the Pryse family, George Brunk, and the Mt. Jefferson summit register indicates that Pryse and Wolfe did not climb The Pinnacle. Their probable high point was the ridge just north of The Pinnacle. This does not diminish their accomplishment, but mountaineering tradition does deny them the credit for completing the first ascent.

9 North Ridge

The North Ridge is the obvious arete which separates Whitewater Glacier from Jefferson Park Glacier. It is quite prominent and sharp from about 8,600 feet to about 9,500 feet. Above 9,500 feet, the ridge fades and blends into the northeast shoulder of the mountain. With a protective layer of snow or ice on the upper section of the route, the North Ridge is relatively safe. Without the benefit of a frozen cover, rockfall constantly rakes the upper section, and the climbing is scary fourth-or fifth-class on rotten rock.

Start from Jefferson Park. Climb up to 9,000 feet on Jefferson Park Glacier. Some parties gain the Ridge here and follow the crest until it fades into the upper face. If there is enough snow, continue up Jefferson Park Glacier and traverse up and left onto the steep face. Near the top, contour left around vertical cliffs and onto the east face. Follow the first convenient gully to the summit rim. Continue south toward the summit. Traverse right around, or go directly over, a small outcrop. Continue on to the base of The Pinnacle.

FA: Sidney S. Mohler, August 9, 1903. Contemporary accounts of Sidney Mohler's climb appeared in three newspapers: the *Statesman* of Aug. 27, 1903, the *Oregon City Courier* of Aug. 28. 1903, and the *Oregon City Enterprise* of Aug. 28, 1903. The Courier gives the date of Mohler's climb as August 9, 1903, but details of his route of ascent are missing from all three accounts. The *Courier* and *Statesman* both mention that Mohler found no evidence that anyone had preceded him, except for two unfinished arrowheads. He was unable to find a Mazama summit register, which was left on top of The Pinnacle in 1897. Mohler did plant a two-foot flagpole which was found later by other parties (*Journal* 1907).

Since details of Mohler's route up Jefferson are missing from the newspapers, the only written clue as to where he climbed appears in *Mazama* (1905).

> *There are three ridges on the north side of Mt. Jefferson,*
> *between which are impassable glaciers seamed with deadly crevasses,*
> *so that the ridge selected by the climber must be adhered to until the*
> *summit is reached. The north ridge which Mr. Mohler ascended in*

Mt. Jefferson from the North　　　　　　　　　　*Terry Toedtemeier photo*

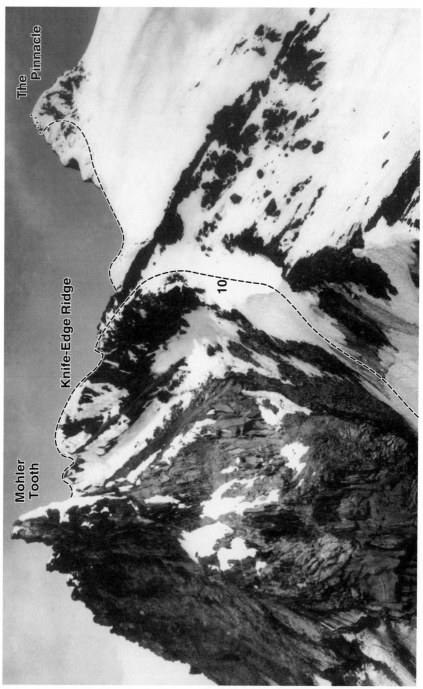

Upper Section of Jefferson Park Glacier route   *Fred H. Kiser (1907) photo*

1903 is one to be avoided, according to his reports, since near the top there are many precipitous cliffs composed of loose, rolling rocks. Therefore the middle ridge was selected by Mr. Mohler for this second ascent (in 1905).

Recently a photo by S.S. Mohler has come to light which proves conclusively that Mohler was on the north ridge. The picture is of a unique rock spire which still sits about halfway up the ridge.

10 Jefferson Park Glacier

Jefferson Park Glacier is the most interesting route on Mt. Jefferson, with snow and ice climbing on the glacier, and easy (5.1) fifth-class climbing on a knife-edge ridge just south of the Mohler Tooth. Camp either in Jefferson Park, or, to shorten the approach in the morning, on one of two moraines leading up to the left (east) side of Jefferson Park Glacier. Sites can be found all the way up the moraines, but they deteriorate after leaving the krumholtz (stunted trees).

Follow either moraine to the east side of the Glacier. Continue up the glacier toward the bergschrund, just below the saddle between Smith Rock and the Mohler Tooth. In the past 10 years, a second bergschrund has appeared. The later in the season the climb is attempted, the more difficult it will be to cross both successfully. Cross the bergschrunds on snow bridges if at all possible. If not, bypass the schrund by rock climbing on the extreme left or right sides. The route on the left starts low, then follows a thin ledge which ends above the schrund.

If you choose to climb the bergschrund on the left side, beware. The rock cliffs above are rotten, and rockfall is probable. Be especially cautious if there are climbers above. Anything they might knock off will come down on top of you.

A 40-to 45-degree slope leads to the col after passing the bergschrund. From the col follow the ridge leading east. At one point the ridge crest narrows. You must either stay on top of the ridge or traverse its southwest side. Both variations are technically easy (5.1), except the ridge is composed of large loose blocks. The blocks themselves are solid, but it is not always obvious what is holding some of them in place. When covered with snow and ice, both variations are quite challenging. With or without snow the exposure is enormous.

After the knife-edge continue on to the main north-south ridge leading to The Pinnacle. Time from Jefferson Park, 7-10 hours.

FRA: Carl Kurath and A.B. Metcalf, Aug. 22, 1931 (Scott 1933). They skirted the bergschrund and much of the steeper ice by climbing rock off to the right of the upper glacier. Kurath and Metcalf were probably not the first individuals to complete the route. There are at least four other parties in the summit register which may have climbed Jefferson Park Glacier earlier than 1931. It proved impossible to determine exactly what route these parties climbed. The first direct ascent of the glacier, without resorting to rock climbing off to either side, was probably by Everett Darr, Jim Mount, and Barney Macnab on Sept. 4, 1933.

11 Russell Glacier

Russell Glacier is an easier but longer alternative to Jefferson Park Glacier. Approach from Jefferson Park or a high bivouac below Jefferson Park Glacier.

From Jefferson Park, gain the east lateral moraine of Jefferson Park Glacier. Follow the moraine until it looks feasible to cross over to the west lateral moraine, which was once a medial moraine for both Jefferson Park and Russell Glaciers. Continue up to the head of Russell Glacier and climb an easy headwall. Turn left and follow a ridge up past the Prehistoric Monster. Skirt the south side of Smith Rock and gain the col above Jefferson Park Glacier. Continue on the Jefferson Park Glacier route, past the crux knife-edge to the summit.

Variation 11A. The ridge above Russell glacier can also be gained from the west. From a bivouac somewhere above the Skyline Trail, proceed up wooded slopes to timberline. Gain the ridge and follow it south and east.

FA via Variation 11A: Lucius J. Hicks and Sidney S. Mohler, August 14, 1906. An article in *Mazama* (1907) describes this route. The article is very confusing, but a careful reader will be able to discern what occurred. A photo with a line drawing, which did not appear in the article, but which did appear in the Mazama annual outing prospectus for 1907, clearly shows the lower portion of the route.

Like the sourdoughs on Denali, Mohler and Hicks somehow wrestled up the route and "planted securely in the rocks a flagstaff twelve feet long with their names and the date engraved at its base" (Mazama 1907). The wooden pole is visible in many older pictures of the summit, but it was destroyed when lightning struck the top of The Pinnacle and blew off several feet of rock in 1937. Mohler seems to have preferred this method of signing in, as he also brought a smaller pole to the summit in 1903.

12 North Milk Creek Gully

North Milk Creek Gully can be a fast climb on firm snow. From trailhead to summit, it is one of the shortest routes on Mt. Jefferson. Do not try to climb the Gully after the snow has melted, unless you enjoy loose scree, rockfall, and waterfalls. The waterfalls are deathtraps just before they melt out and become visible. The North Milk Creek Glacier is probably gone (see Description).

Follow a short connector trail west and north from Pamelia Lake to its intersection with the PCT in Milk Creek Canyon. Follow a climbers' trail up Milk Creek Canyon to the first fork in Milk Creek. Gain the top of the ridge separating the two creeks and follow it to timberline. Good bivy sites will be found in the heather above the trees. Climb the steep slopes into the North Milk Creek Cirque, then move south to the northern base of The Pinnacle.

FA: Andrew Montgomery and William Montgomery. August 24, 1914 (J; Montgomery, William 1984; Montgomery, Bernard 1984).

13 West Rib

The West Rib is an obvious ridge, separated by two large gullies on the west face of Mt. Jefferson. The Rib is the shortest route to The Pinnacle. Well-

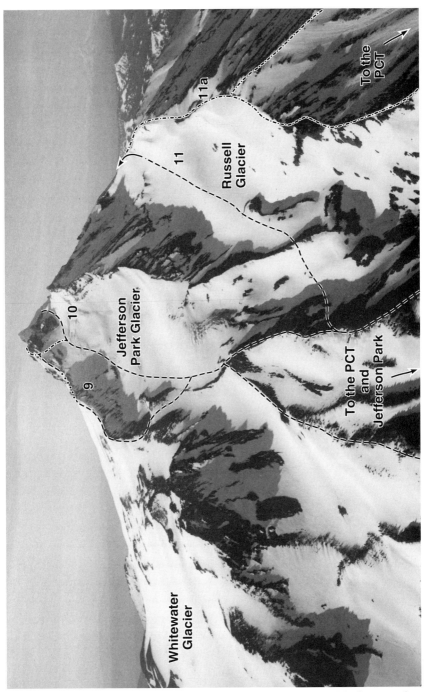

Mt. Jefferson from the North

Terry Toedtemeier photo

Mt. Jefferson from the West   *Don Lowe photo*

conditioned climbers use the West Rib for one-day climbs of Jefferson during the winter or early spring. Because the Rib is exposed to the wind, it is usually free of snow by late spring. Without snow, the West Rib is a boring slog up steep scree.

Follow a short connector trail west and north from Pamelia Lake to its intersection with the PCT in Milk Creek Canyon. Follow a climbers' trail up Milk Creek Canyon to the first fork in Milk Creek. Gain the top of the ridge separating the two creeks and follow it to timberline. Gain the West Rib and follow it to the base of The Pinnacle.

FA: Mr. and Mrs. W.E. Stone, August 14, 1917 (J). Arthur P. McKinlay and his party attained the base of The Pinnacle in 1901, basically by the route that the Stones used. McKinlay did not climb The Pinnacle (*Evening Telegram* 1901).

14 South Milk Creek Gully

Approach as for the West Rib and North Milk Creek Gully. Climb the Gully. Not recommended.

Climbers on the summit pinnacle, Three Fingered Jack   *John Lindstrom photo*

THREE FINGERED JACK (7,841')

Within minutes, six elated young Central Oregonians straddled the knife-edged summit of Three Fingered Jack....McNeal did a handstand on the crest and let out another loud yodel. The acrobatics surely unnerved his friends, for there was no room for him to return to his feet except in precisely perfect form.

Don Alan Hall on Ervin McNeal's summit ritual in 1923

DESCRIPTION

Three Fingered Jack is about 14 miles due south of Mt. Jefferson and about four miles north of Santiam Pass. The highest point on Three Fingered Jack is unmistakable from the east or west. So is the northwest ridge, which has four or five towers large enough to be seen from a distance. Perhaps some combination of the summit and two of these towers gave rise to the name Three Fingered Jack. McArthur (1982) was, "unable to learn who named it or when."

Unless you want to climb the South Ridge, stay away from Three Fingered Jack. The remaining lines pass through a treacherous mixture of basalt flow and pyroclastic debris. Several routes do have the potential for good winter climbing, but the trick is finding them in the proper condition.

MAPS

The following maps are currently (1991) available for Three Fingered Jack.
1. Three Fingered Jack, 7.5 minute quadrangle, published by USGS in 1988.
2. Mt. Jefferson Wilderness, published by the USFS in 1979.

ROADS AND TRAILS

The PCT. The PCT is the best approach to the South Ridge, the West Face, and the Northwest Ridge of Three Fingered Jack. Some climbers prefer to approach the South Ridge from Square Lake and Booth Lake, but the USFS has blocked the old trailhead and prefers the public to use the new PCT trailhead.

Follow U.S. Highway 20-126 to Santiam Pass. Between the summit sign and the Hoodoo Ski Bowl and Big Lake road, turn north at the well-marked entrance to the PCT trailhead. Drive four tenths of a mile and park.

Follow the PCT north for approximately five to six miles or two to three hours.

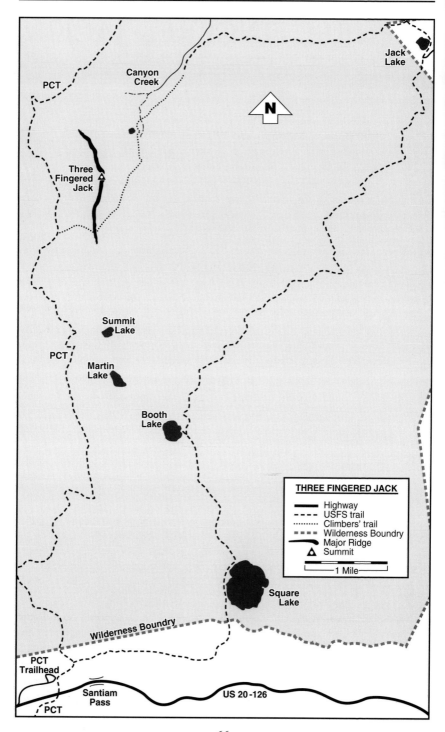

Canyon Creek

PCT

Jack Lake

N

Three Fingered Jack

Summit Lake

PCT

Martin Lake

Booth Lake

THREE FINGERED JACK

━━━ Highway
- - - USFS trail
········ Climbers' trail
▬▬▬ Wilderness Boundry
⌒ Major Ridge
△ Summit

━1 Mile━

Square Lake

Wilderness Boundry

PCT Trailhead

Santiam Pass

US 20-126

PCT

Not long after the west side of Three Fingered Jack becomes visible, but before the PCT leaves the trees, follow a climbers' trail right and uphill into the woods.

Jack Lake Road (USFS 12) and Canyon Creek Meadow Trail. Use Jack Lake Road and Canyon Creek Meadow Trail to reach the east side of Three Fingered Jack and as an alternative approach to the South Ridge.

Seven miles east of Santiam Pass or about 12 miles northwest of Sisters, turn north off Highway 20-126 onto Jack Lake Road (USFS 12). Drive about 4.5 miles to USFS 1230 where the pavement ends. Bear left on 1230 and drive 1.6 miles to USFS 1234. Stay left on 1234 and drive six miles to Jack Lake. The road is well gravelled and well marked.

From Jack Lake, follow the Canyon Creek Meadow and Wasco Lake trail about 10 minutes to the Mt. Jefferson Wilderness boundary, where the trail forks. Stay left on the trail to Canyon Creek Meadow. Once in the meadow, continue up the trail to a gap in an old terminal moraine to reach the Northeast Face. Attain the South Ridge by following the moraine up and left to a low point in the east ridge, and contouring across scree to the south. Time to the moraine, 1-2 hours.

Winter Access. Park in the Santiam Snow Play snow park area near the Hoodoo Ski Bowl and Big Lake turnoff. Head east about one mile, and follow the PCT, which is usually well skied-out during most of the season. Alternatively, ski east past the PCT. Continue on to Square Lake. Head north about two-and-one-half miles on an unmarked trail past Booth Lake. Leave the trail and climb up to timberline and the southeast bowl of Three Fingered Jack.

DESCENT

Descend down the South Ridge. See that route for particulars.

ROUTES

1 South Ridge

The South Ridge is the only recommended route on Three Fingered Jack. Despite its share of loose rock, it is enjoyable and relatively safe. There is actually very little climbing involved except for two short pitches near the top. Bring a rope and use it on these pitches, as there is considerable exposure and risk.

Follow the PCT north for roughly five to six miles or two to three hours. Not long after the west side of Three Fingered Jack becomes visible, but before the PCT leaves the trees, a climbers' trail, marked by a rock cairn, cuts right uphill into the woods. The trail steepens and emerges onto a treeless hillside, marked by a conspicuous scar. The scar is the result of climbers trying to get down from Three Fingered Jack quickly. Do not follow the scar or several trails above it which diagonal up and left toward the summit. It is quicker and less tiring to continue straight up along the forest edge toward a low point in the South Ridge. (During the descent it is quicker to plunge-step down the scree on the treeless hillside).

Hike up the south ridge, passing several gendarmes on the left. Near the summit, a large gendarme which appears to block further progress can be passed on the right via a sloping ledge (5.1). The ledge is overhung by the gendarme wall on the west and drops 800 feet on the east, so people get down on all fours to try and get by. Because of this, the ledge is called The Crawl. The hardest part of the climb comes at the end of the ledge, where you must get up off your knees and use your feet. Fortunately, the rock is some of the best found anywhere on the mountain.

After the gendarme, continue up past an eight-foot vertical wall to the base of the summit pinnacle. Climb an obvious chimney or groove, using whatever appears most solid. If you need protection, bring nuts or camming devices in the 1" range for a crack on the right side of the chimney. Finish up horrid rock to the summit, a somewhat terrifying mixture of cinders and cobbles which probably does vibrate in the wind as the original ascent party claimed. The view is spectacular.

To descend, downclimb or rappel the route. Sometimes there are no fixed rappel points, so come prepared with extra sling if downclimbing is not your forte.

FA of South Ridge and Three Fingered Jack: Ervin D. McNeal, Armin E. Furrer, Phil M. Philbrook, Elmer Johnson, Leo Harryman, and Ernest R. Putnam, Sept. 3, 1923 (*Bend Bulletin* 1923).

FWA of the South Ridge and of Three Fingered Jack: Norlin B. Wolfe, Bob Hunter, and Verlin M. Wolfe, March 23, 1941 (3FJ).

Other variations up the final 100 feet of the pinnacle include the northeast face by Bill Unsoeld, Gudmund Kaarhus, Norman Lee, Bill McCracken, and Phyllis Hinson, June 16, 1947 (3FJ); the south face via a 150-foot chimney by Jack Zimmerman and Phil Sorensen, July 29, 1951 (3FJ); and the west face by Art Johnson, Norman Lee, and John Skillern, July 11, 1952 (3FJ). These variations all have rotten rock and are not recommended.

2 Southeast Couloir

The Southeast Couloir is an 800-foot gully which ends just above The Crawl. Approach from either the PCT or Square Lake. Avoid the slope beneath the Southeast Couloir if avalanche danger is high. This slope is on the leeward side of the South Ridge, and generates a number of slides. The first 150 feet of the route is the crux. During the first ascent, Bob Bauman found 5.6 moves on 65-degree rotten rock. During the second ascent, Tom and Bob Bauman found solid water ice. The rest of the couloir is 45 to 50 degrees. Stay to the sides of the gully to avoid rockfall, especially if the weather is warm.

FA: Bob Bauman, April 14, 1970 (3FJ).

3 Northeast Face

The rock is so soft in places that the second ascent party was able to chop steps with an ice ax. In good conditions this might be a good winter climb. Approach from Jack Lake Road and Canyon Creek Meadow. Not recommended.

FA: Charlie Bell, Eric Beck, and Stuart Ferguson, Summer 1960 (Dodge 1975).

4 Northwest Ridge

The rock is rotten, and the route is contrived and overlong. Approach from either Jack Lake or the PCT. Begin at the far end of the Ridge and climb to the summit over every intervening gendarme. Several gendarmes cannot be climbed from the north, but must be passed on the west and climbed from the west or south. Not recommended.

FA: Everett Darr, Ida Darr, and Eldon Metzger, Sept. 6, 1942 (3FJ). Darr stated in a 1970 interview that, "we tried to stay on the pinnacles best as possible" (Hall 1975).

5 Northwest Face

The rock is very poor and the route is seldom done. Approach via the PCT. Pass the climbers' trail to the South Ridge and continue north past Three Fingered Jack's highest summit. Slog up 1,000 feet of scree to a point just north of a light-colored rib of rock northwest of the summit. Work up diagonally across broad ledges with an occasional fifth-class move (5.4). Gain the north ridge just below the summit and follow it to the top.

FA: Everett Darr and Joe Leuthold, June 22, 1941. They wrote:

> *Up west face at middle finger-side trip to top of Aguille (surmise it is the middle finger located a few hundred feet north of here). Don't advise it as a party climb.* (3FJ)

6 West Face Direct

If you want to repeat this route, consider this description.

> *ROCK APES 4:00 pm. First Ascent-W. Face direct from bottom. 5 1/2 hrs. on rock. First 300 feet cramponing on horrible rock-pitons driven straight into rock. Crux pitch consisted of 3 direct aid pins to a 9" ledge then an exciting free move on an overhang using barely stable holds. Scrambled to basalt buttress to join Ted Davis's 'first' on the upper face. Climb ended in a 25 ft. jam and knob climb just north of summit. Bob Bauman-right hand covered with blood (so is the rope, pins, biners, etc, etc, etc,), Mark McLaughlin-Obsidians Eugene Oregon.* (3FJ)

Variation 6A: West Face. Hike up the South Ridge to just above the first large gendarmes. Traverse north horizontally. Climb a gully and several rock ribs which lead toward the summit pinnacle. Scramble 100 feet up the north side of the summit. Not recommended.

FA: Bob Bauman and Mark McLaughlin, June 5, 1966.

FWA: Tom Blust and Kent Benesch, winter 1982 (Blust 1988).

FA of Variation, Bill Cummins and Ted Davis, Oct. 24, 1964.

Tom Bauman on the crux of the East Buttress   *Alan Kearney photo*

MT. WASHINGTON (7,794')

*Among others was a solitary tower, or needle, of basalt,
many hundreds of feet high, standing by itself at the foot of the
mountains, like some grim sentinel at the foot of Olympian
heights.*

George L. Woods observing Mt. Washington from North Sister in 1857

DESCRIPTION

Mount Washington is an isolated basalt pinnacle on the crest of the Cascades between Santiam and McKenzie Passes. Three prominent ridges radiate north, west and south from the base of the pinnacle. Large snowfields sometimes prevail on the east and west sides into July, but there are no glaciers or remnant glaciers.

Evidence suggests that the name Mt. Washington probably originated during construction of the Willamette Valley and Cascade Mountain Military Road. The road was built from Sweet Home east over Santiam Pass, and into Central Oregon, and was completed in 1867. A series of four maps were prepared by surveyor James A. Warner which showed the road in relation to surrounding features. Clearly labeled on the first map, and located several miles south of the Pass, is "Washingtons Peak" (Oregon State Archives 1871).

Mount Washington was originally formed as a shield volcano. Later, basalt invaded the shield and formed a basalt plug. Pleistocene glaciation stripped the outer debris, leaving the plug much as we see it today. Rock quality varies, but the west face, west ridge, south face, southeast ridge, and east buttress all have good rock. Indeed, Mount Washington is the only place in the Oregon Cascades where the alpine rock climber might find happiness.

The best time to climb Mount Washington is late spring, summer, and early fall. The approach, the climb, and the return can easily be done in a day. Winter ascents usually take two days.

Water is difficult to find in late summer and fall, the only year-round source being Coldwater Spring (see approach). Hard hats are recommended, and you must wear them if a party is climbing above you. Take ice axe and crampons between November and June. The decision whether to take rock shoes or mountain boots depends on season and individual preference.

MAPS

The following maps are currently (1991) available for Mt. Washington.
1. Mt. Washington, 7.5 minute quadrangle, published by USGS in 1988.
2. Mt. Washington Wilderness, published by the USFS in 1973.

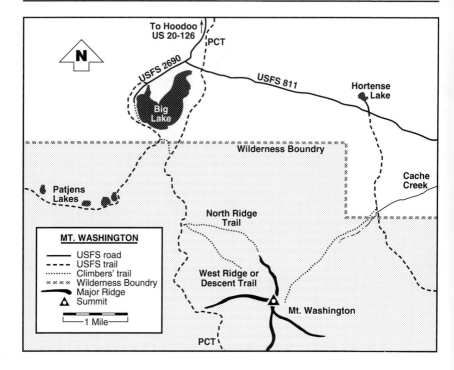

ROADS AND TRAILS

Hoodoo and Big Lake Road (USFS 2690) and the PCT. This route is the easiest way to reach Mt. Washington. Follow U.S 20-126 to the Hoodoo Ski Bowl and Big Lake turnoff one mile west of Santiam Pass. Turn south off U.S. 20-126 toward Hoodoo Ski Bowl on USFS 2690. Follow USFS 2690 4.2 miles to a trailhead on the west side of Big Lake. To reach the base of the climbs:

1. Follow an unmarked trail along the lake for two or three minutes, to a junction with a second trail called the Patjens Lake Trail.

2. Continue around Big Lake until the trail leaves the shoreline.

3. At an obvious junction, turn left (east). (Continuing straight will lead away from Mt. Washington to Patjens Lake.) Head east for about five minutes. Several spur trails will join the trail from the west, but continue east until the trail splits.

4. Take the right fork for two or three minutes to a clearing with a pile of dead logs on its south side. (The left fork continues around the east side of Big Lake).

5. Turn right (south) in the clearing and follow a wide trail for five minutes to its junction with the Pacific Crest Trail (PCT).

6. Follow the PCT south for 30 minutes (or about one hour from the roadhead), to a climbers' trail which goes uphill to the east. The climbers' trail is usually marked by a cairn and is just after a large rock on the left side of the trail. If you reach Coldwater Spring, the only year-round water source on this section of the PCT, you have missed the climbers' trail and hiked about 10 minutes too far.

7. About 150 feet after leaving the PCT, the climbers' trail splits. The right fork can be used for gaining the west ridge or routes on the south face. Follow the left fork until it breaks out of the timber onto the north ridge proper. Drop onto the east side and contour around the base of the North Ridge for routes on the east face. Continue up the ridge for routes on the north and west faces.

Hoodoo and Big Lake Rd (USFS 2690), USFS 811, Hortense Lake Trail and Cache Creek. This route is an alternative and perhaps easier way to the east face of Mt. Washington. Follow U.S 20-126 to the Hoodoo Ski Bowl and Big Lake turnoff, one mile west of the Santiam Pass sign. Turn south on USFS 2690 and drive about three miles. Turn left (east) on USFS 811, and follow a rough dirt road three miles to Hortense Lake. Follow a trail south about two miles to Cache Creek. Leave the trail and travel cross-country up Cache Creek and through meadows above to the east side.

DESCENT

The only recommended route off the summit pinnacle is down the North Ridge. Descend northeast toward Black Butte, a prominent, rounded cinder cone in Central Oregon. After about 100 feet, cut west to a short 10-foot chimney. Continue down easy rock and scree about 250 feet to a large boulder with rappel slings. If you don't mind downclimbing easy rock, use one rope to rappel. Take two ropes to reach all the way to the notch in the north ridge. Glissade or run scree (depending on season) down the west side, and follow a climbers' trail to the PCT.

ROUTES

1 North Ridge (I-5.1)

The North Ridge will never be an award-winning climb. The first pitch is OK, but you find yourself asking, just how good are those holds? The second and third pitches have no more fascination than any other slope of decomposing lava. If the North Ridge were not the easiest way to reach the summit of Mt. Washington, this route would be ignored.

Follow the North Ridge climbers' trail from the PCT. As you approach the summit pinnacle, stay on top of the ridge as long as possible. Skirt several towers to the west until you reach the north wall of the summit pinnacle. Move up a short loose gully to a notch just below the northeast side of the mountain.

1. Move right (west) 30 feet and scramble up to a fractured ramp. Climb the ramp up and left 35 feet to the base of a rotten chimney. Climb the chimney and move left, then up, to a ledge with a large block. The block usually contains one or more rappel slings for the descent.

2. & 3. About 250 feet of scrambling leads to a second chimney. From the top of the chimney, scramble 100 feet to the summit. Time from Big Lake, 3-5 hours.

Variation 1A (5.7). From the base of the fractured ramp, climb straight up a zone of good rock (50 feet), then rejoin the regular route. Not recommended.

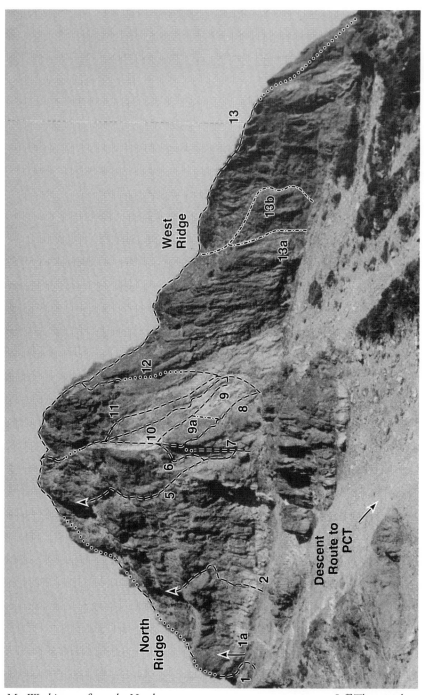

Mt. Washington from the Northwest   *Jeff Thomas photo*

FA: Ervin McNeal, Phil Philbrook, Armin Furrer, Wilbur Watkins, Leo Harryman, and Ronald Sellers, otherwise known as the "Boys from Bend," August 26, 1923 (Sellers 1923). The Boys traversed left from the notch and climbed a ramp or chimney on the east face to reach the scrambling up above. According to Don Onthank, climbers abandoned the chimney in the 1950s because most of it had disappeared (Hall 1975).

FA current first pitch: Nels Skjersaa and Emil Nordeen, 1925 (Johnson 1931).

FWA of route and mountain: Jim Harrang, Bill Byrd, Dr. Ed Keller, and Eugene Sehbring, Feb. 10, 1952 (Harrang 1985).

FA of variation: Bob and Tom Bauman, date unknown (Bauman, Bob 1986).

Fastest known time from west side of Big Lake to summit, 1 hour 8 minutes 36 seconds, Tom Blust, summer 1984 (Blust 1988).

2 North Face, Center (II-5.8)

Start in the middle of the north face below a large right-facing dihedral. Climb up 40 feet to an overhang just under the dihedral.

Move right 20 feet, climb up several feet, then traverse back left 20 feet to the base of the dihedral. Climb dihedral until forced to diagonal up and right to the base of an overhang. Climb the overhang and belay above. Rope drag is hard to avoid and protection is hard to find. Not recommended.

FA: Bob and Tom Bauman, July 16, 1967 (Bauman, Tom 1981).

3 North Face, Right

A Mazama summit register contains the following entry.

> *Climbed North Face beginning approx. 200 ft. to the east of the West buttress or 2-300 yds west of the conventional NE Route. 12 pitons were used for security. The belay points were somewhat limited but sufficient. Harrangs form was unexcelled. The weather was most generous.*

Several climbers, with the summit register entry in hand, spent the better part of a day trying to find the route. This proved futile. The first ascent party was unable to pinpoint the route during separate interviews.

FA: Jim Harrang, Art Johnson, August 26, 1951.

4 North Face, Unsoeld-Moffit Route

Willi Unsoeld wrote, "Ascent by route lying just to the left of N.W. buttress" (W). It is conceivable that Unsoeld and Moffit climbed the 1945 line of Petrie, Pearson, Margosian, and Edmunds, but there is not enough detail in the summit register description to tell one from another. During an interview, Robert Moffit was unable to place the route. A detailed letter from Willi Unsoeld also could not place the route.

FA: Willi Unsoeld and Robert A. Moffit, July 20, 1947.

5 Northwest Dihedral, Left Side (II-5.6)

The route described here is the original 1945 route. Two climbers used photos taken by Dave Pearson on the first ascent to locate the line. Belay 30 feet up from the scree on a ledge at the base of the Northwest Dihedral, or belay 15 feet lower under an overhang to protect the belayer from rockfall.

1. Climb up center of dihedral for 20 feet until it is possible to traverse up and left to a groove. Climb 30 feet up the groove to easy ground, and belay.

2. Above the belay are two right-facing dihedrals. Follow the left-hand dihedral and exit right at the top. Belay 10 feet higher on a ledge.

3.& 4. Scramble to top.

FA: Dave Pearson, Ross Petrie, Leon Margosian, and Arthur Edmunds, Sept. 2, 1945 (W). Pearson lead both pitches because Petrie had brought tricounis. Tennis shoes were not common, and Ross thought of Washington as a "boot" climb.

6 Cling To The Earth (II-5.10c)

Belay on a ledge at the base of the Northwest Dihedral, or belay 15 feet lower under an overhang to protect the belayer from rockfall.

1. Climb center of dihedral for 90 feet. Climb over a roof. Undercling up and right under a second roof to the second belay on the West Face.

2. Follow the West Face, or rappel (two ropes are needed).

FA: Bob McGown and Tim Olson, June 1987 (Olson 1989).

7 Northwest Dihedral, Right Side (II-5.8)

Belay on a ledge at the base of the Northwest Dihedral, or belay 15 feet lower under an overhang to protect the belayer from rockfall.

1. Climb 65 feet up a shallow dihedral four feet right of the main dihedral. Just before an overhang, face climb right and slightly down (crux) for 25 feet. Climb up to the second belay on the West Face. The traverse is hard to protect.

2. Follow the West Face or rappel (two ropes are needed).

FA: Bob Bauman, July 31, 1966 (W).

8 Northwest Dihedral, Outside Edge (II-5.9)

Start on a rib of rock on the left side of the west face.

1. Scramble 60 feet to the bottom of an overhanging dihedral. Follow the dihedral up and left 70 feet to a ceiling. Pass the ceiling on the right. Climb straight up to the second belay for the West Face.

2. Follow the West Face or rappel (two ropes are needed).

FA: Bob Bauman and Ken Jern, August 12, 1966 (W).

9 West Face (II-5.6)

A excellent route. Smaller nuts down to 1/4" are useful on the third pitch.

1. Start on the left side of the west face. Climb up and right on fractured blocks. until directly below a prominent left-facing dihedral. Climb up to a small belay stance about 10 feet below the start of the prominent dihedral.

Mt. Washington West Face   *Jeff Thomas photo*

2. Face-climb up and left 120 feet to a good belay ledge.

3. Follow a prominent white corner (5.9) directly above the belay, or face-climb to the right of the corner (5.6). Both lead to a rubble-filled gully. Warning: be careful not to knock rocks loose in the gully; your belayer is directly below.

4.& 5. Scramble about 250 feet up the right wall of the gully and along the West Ridge to the summit.

Variation 9A: Heart of Stone (5.10 D). From the base, climb up to a thin seam which starts just to the right of Northwest Corner Outside Edge. Follow the seam up to the second pitch on the West Face. Climb up and left to a good belay. Rappel or finish up the West Face.

FA: Jim Harrang and Jack Meyer, September 18, 1952 (W).

FFA: probably Pat Callis and Gerry Honey, July 5, 1958. During a phone interview Callis confirmed that they climbed the route without aid (Callis 1986).

FA: Heart of Stone Bob McGown and Tim Olson, June 1987 (Olson 1989).

10 King Rat (II-5.9+)

A steep route with a wild crux. Protection on the lower, more difficult half of the second pitch is good, but the top, easier half of the second pitch is a runout.

1. Climb and belay as for the West Face.

2. Move right, and climb up to a steep left-facing dihedral. Follow the dihedral. The crux is a traverse under an overlap. When the dihedral ends, continue face-climbing straight up to a rubble-filled gully.

3. & 4. Scramble about 250 feet up the right wall of the gully and along the West Ridge to the summit.

FA: Tom Bauman, Dennis Root, and Jim Newman, 1979 (Bauman, T. 1986).

11 Central Pillar (II-5.8+)

Steep, exposed, and a joy to climb. There are several 15-and-20 foot runouts, but the crux is well protected. Take a #4 Friend or its equivalent.

1. Climb diagonal ramps toward the right side of the west face. Belay on small ledges above the first belay for the West Face and next to an obvious crack which diagonals up and left.

2. Move left into crack and follow it 40 feet to its end on top of a block. Move right off the block and then face-climb straight up 110 feet to small belay ledges.

3.& 4. Move up 20 feet into a debris-filled gully. Scramble about 250 feet up the right wall of the gully and along the West Ridge to the summit.

FA: Tom Bauman, Ken Keeling, and Bob Freund, 1976 (Bauman, T. 1986).

12 Chimney of Space (II-5.8)

1. Start up the same diagonal ramp system used for other routes on the west face. The first pitch ends on small ledges just below the chimney.

2. Gain chimney (crux) and follow 140 feet to a belay atop a pedestal.

3. Climb 130 feet to the top of the west ridge.

4. Scramble to the summit.

FA: Bob and Tom Bauman, July 16, 1967 (W).

13 West Ridge (II-5.8)

The West Ridge can be climbed from the north, west, and south. The first ascent party climbed the North Wall (See Variations). The rock on their route is rotten. Currently, most parties gain the West Ridge from its lower western toe. The climbing at the bottom of this route is excellent, but pitches two and three traverse the unstable Cascade Dinner Plates. Some parties climb the South Wall to gain the West Ridge (See Variations). The South Wall avoids the Dinner Plates, and is especially attractive during cold weather because of its southern exposure.

After leaving the PCT, follow the climbers' trail and take the right fork up to and through the west-side meadows. At the base of the west face scree slope, cut south to the west ridge and follow it to where the rock begins. The route begins at a distinct notch just up from the bottom of the West Ridge. Gain the notch from the south via fourth-class slabs or by moderate fifth-class climbing from the north.

1. From the notch, traverse up and right 10 feet into a groove. Surprisingly difficult crack climbing (5.7 or 5.8) leads to easier ground. Continue a full rope length to secure belay ledges.

2.& 3. Follow an easy (fourth class) but scary section of ridge for the next 250 feet. Large precarious flakes, called The Cascade Dinner Plates, line the top. Like all fine china, the Plates must be handled with care. Belay at a small rock step.

4. Continue up the ridge and belay at the base of the pinnacle proper.

5. Climb up to a V-shaped chimney. Climb to the top of the chimney (5.6), and continue another 40 feet to a good belay.

6.& 7. Amble up easy rock to the summit. Time from Big Lake, 6 to 7 hours.

Variation 13A: Jern's Call (5.7). Scramble up scree on the north side of the west ridge. Start about three-quarters of the way up from the toe of the west ridge. Climb an overhang and gain a right-facing corner. Follow the corner to the ridge. Poor protection. Not recommended.

Variation 13B: North Wall (5.6). Scramble up scree on the north side of the west ridge. Start about halfway between the toe of the west ridge and the start of the West Face. Climb up to the crest of the ridge and join the regular route. Alternatively, if you wish to avoid the Cascade Dinner Plates, climb up about 50 feet, and traverse left (east) and up, paralleling the crest of the ridge. Move up to the crest of the ridge just before a small step.

Variation 13C: South Wall (5.6). Hike up the south side of the west ridge several hundred feet. Start at a crack system which appears to lead toward a point where the crest of the west ridge steepens abruptly. Follow cracks for about 200 feet. Where the cracks disappear, continue straight up easier but poorer quality rock to the regular route. This variation is highly recommended.

FA of North Wall: Ross Petrie, Leo Margosian, and David Pearson, September 13, 1947 (W; Margosian 1947).

FA of regular route: probably Gudman Kaarhus, Silver (Norm) Lee, and Ralph W. Johnson, July 30, 1950 (W).

FA of Jern's Call: Ken Jern and Bob Bauman, August 11, 1966 (W, Obsidian).

FA of South Wall: unknown.

14 Southwest Face (II-5.7)

The Southwest has lots of fractured rock and stacked debris piles. One climber has stated that so much rock fell off during his ascent, that whoever followed him would be doing a new route. Not recommended.

FA: Dale Kunz and Laurel Berg October 4, 1952 (W).

Mt. Washington South Face   *Jeff Thomas photo*

15 South Face Dihedral (II-5.7)

The first pitch is one of the best on Washington. The top two pitches are so-so. After leaving the PCT, follow the climbers' trail until it forks. Take the right fork up to and through the west-side meadows. At the base of the west-face scree slope, cut south to the west ridge and follow it to where the rock begins. Swing around to the south side of the rock, and scramble up a long scree slope to the top of the south ridge. Begin just west of the east-side dropoff, below an obvious dihedral.

1. Climb dihedral about 70 feet. Move across a blank section under a ceiling (crux), and continue 80 feet. Belay. You can also break this lead in two and belay just above the crux on a good ledge.

2. Continue straight up on easy ground, then climb a large face on the right.

3. Scramble to the summit.

Variation 15A (5.9). Start about 20 feet left of the the South Face Dihedral and climb directly up, paralleling the dihedral for 140 feet. Follow the last two pitches of the South Face Dihedral.

FRA: Bob Bauman and Ron Funke, July 1966. Several parties might have climbed the the South Face Dihedral in the late 1940s and early 1950s, but their summit register entries are vague. During separate interviews in the 1980s, they could not remember exactly what route they climbed.

FA of Variation 15A: Steve Lyford and Tom Blust, Oct. 16, 1976 (Blust 1988).

16 South Face (II-5.8)

Start at the base of the South Face Dihedral.

1. Climb South Face Dihedral for 70 feet. Belay.

2. Climb an overhanging corner up and right for approximately 10 feet (crux). Belay at the first convenient spot.

3. & 4. Scramble to the top.

FA: Eldon Metzger, Ralph Calkin, Jim Mount, Everett and Ida Darr, June 8, 1940 (*Mazama* 1940). The South Face is an historically significant climb. Eldon Metzger drove seven pitons for direct aid at the beginning of the second pitch (Metzger 1981). Thus, the South Face is the first climb in Oregon which relied on pitons for its successful completion.

17 Southeast Spur (III-5.5)

A long moderate climb. The first 200 feet follows good rock on a beautiful ridge. The upper third of the route wanders from one debris-covered ledge to another. Take care on the upper pitches, as anything you knock loose, will funnel down to the approach gully on the East Buttress.

1. & 2. Start at the foot of the ridge. Follow cracks up low-angle slabs.

3., 4., & 5. Easy fourth-class climbing along the ridge leads to a short headwall.

6. Climb the headwall, and continue up steep rock until the first good belay.

7., 8., etc. Several rope lengths of easy fifth-class scrambling lead to the top.

Variation 17A (5.10-). A two-pitch alternative starts on the broad east face of the Southeast Spur about halfway across. The first pitch is rotten and poorly protected, but the second pitch is quite good.

FA: John Lindstrom and Gene Hebert, July 25, 1959 (W).

FA of Variation 17A: Bob McGown and Harvey Schmitt, July 14, 1984.

18 East Buttress (III-5.8)

The buttress is a compelling combination of sound basalt, fun face-climbing, and high exposure. However, you must climb a rotten gully between the Southeast Spur and East Buttress to gain the buttress. Start at the base of this gully.

1.& 2. Climb the rotten gully. When the rock on the right side of the gully begins to noticeably improve in quality, traverse right to a ledge at the base of a steep blocky wall. The gully can be partially snow or completely bare rock depending on season.

3. Move up 10 feet off the belay. Traverse right to the crest of the buttress. The exposure will be nothing less than exhilarating. After gaining the crest of the buttress, move up about 20 feet (5.6 or 5.7) to easier ground. Belay 40 feet higher on a substantial ledge. Rope drag can be a problem unless the leader is careful.

4.& 5. Interesting but easy climbing leads to an obvious headwall.

6. Climb the left edge of the headwall (crux). Belay at the top of the buttress.

7., etc. The remaining distance to the summit is easy but exposed. Some climb unroped, some use the rope. The easiest route to the summit keeps right for 200 feet until the rock on the left eases in angle. Time from Cache Creek 6-8 hours.

Variation 18A. The original ascent party continued up the gully another pitch. Not recommended.

Variation 18B. At the crux, traverse left into the gully and move up until you can regain the buttress. Not recommended.

Variation 18C. Just below the crux, traverse right 35 feet. Climb straight up 30 feet to a small belay. Traverse back left to regain the crest of the buttress.

FA: Tom Bauman & Tom Gann via 18A&C, July 24, 1965 (W, Obsidian).

FA of 5.8 crux: Tom Bauman and partner, July 30, 1967 (Bauman, T. 1986).

FA 18B & **FWA:** Tom & Bob Bauman, Feb. 11, 1968 (Bauman, T. 1986).

FA pitch 3: Tom Rogers & Wayne Arrington, June 20, 1975 (Rogers 1988).

Tom Bauman traversing to the crest of the East Buttress.   *Alan Kearney photo*

19 East Face Direct (III-5.7)

The rock is rotten, and belays are imaginary. Do not climb this route.

FA: Bob Bauman and Mavis (nee Bodhaine) Bauman, May 30, 1968 (W).

20 East Face (III-5.0)

The route is long and easy but the rock is generally poor. Not recommended.

FA: Dave Nelson, Allison (nee Logan) Belcher, Tom Gibbons, and Charlie Carpenter, July 20, 1957 (Gibbons 1957).

Mt. Washington from the East   *Terry Toedtemeier photo*

Climbers on N.E. Shoulder of Prouty Pinnacle, North Sister   *John Lindstrom photo*

THREE SISTERS AND BROKEN TOP

We passed six lakes, four of them being between the mts. we called Three Sisters, though I am at a loss which of the five peaks are the Three Sisters.

Adolph Dekum showing his confusion during an 1883 trip thru the Sisters

OVERALL DESCRIPTION

The Three Sisters region is the quintessential alpine area. There are five peaks over 9,000 feet, including North Sister, Middle Sister, South Sister, Broken Top, and Bachelor Butte, as well as a host of lesser summits. Interspersed throughout are innumerable high lakes, streams, meadows, and forests, most of which have been protected within the boundaries of The Three Sisters Wilderness.

Since five prominent mountains sit in close proximity to one another, the term Three Sisters is technically incorrect. Very likely the name originated in the Willamette Valley, where only three of the five summits can be seen (McArthur 1982).

MAPS

The following maps are currently (1991) available for Three Sisters.

1. North Sister, 7.5 minute quadrangle, published by USGS in 1988. The provisional edition of this map does not show the Glacier Creek trail from White Branch to the PCT.
2. Trout Creek Butte, 7.5 minute quadrangle, published by USGS in 1988. This map is only necessary to parties approaching the Three Sisters from the east side.
3. South Sister, 7.5 minute quadrangle, published by USGS in 1988.
4. Broken Top, 7.5 minute quadrangle, published by USGS in 1988. Parties climbing South Sister from Green Lakes will want this map for the approach.
5. Three Sisters Wilderness, published by the USFS in 1981. According to the USFS, this map will soon be out of print and will not be redone. They are replacing it with the Geo-Graphics map.
6. Geo-Graphics Three Sisters Wilderness Map with Three Sisters Recreation Map, published 1990 by Geo-Graphics of Portland, Oregon.

ROADS AND TRAILS

Mckenzie Pass Highway (242), Frog Camp, Obsidian Trail, Glacier Creek Trail, and Sunshine. This is the easiest way to reach the west side of the Three Sisters. Mckenzie Pass Highway is not plowed during the winter and usually is not open until late spring or early summer.

One tenth of a mile west of milepost 71 on McKenzie Pass Highway, turn south at a sign which says Obsidian Trail. Drive on a gravel road three tenths of a mile to Frog Camp, a USFS campground. Start on the east side of the campground. Follow the Obsidian Trail for nearly four miles. Cross a chaotic lava flow and White Branch, a creek which parallels the south side of the lava. Just after the creek the trail forks. Take the left fork and follow Glacier Creek Trail. Continue on the trail for less than a mile to a junction with the PCT. This area is known as Sunshine, named for Sunshine Shelter which was removed years ago. Follow an unmarked climbers' trail southeast up a small canyon.

Pole Creek Spring Road (USFS 15 and 1524). Pole Creek Spring Road is usually open by late May and provides access to climbs on the east side of North and Middle Sister, and the north side of South Sister.

From the town of Sisters, drive west on Mckenzie Highway (State highway 242) about 1.6 miles to Pole Creek Spring Road (USFS 15). Follow USFS 15 and USFS 1524 almost 11 miles to a parking area and trailhead.

Follow Pole Creek Trail 1.5 miles to the east-side trail junction (USFS trail 96). This trail traverses the length of the Three Sisters from Green Lakes in the south to the PCT in the north. From the junction, travel cross-country due west toward North Sister, moving slightly south of the shoulder of Peak 7355. Depending on snow level, you should be able to reach timberline in about two hours.

Approach Middle Sister by hiking south on the east-side trail (USFS 96) one-half mile to the Chambers Lakes Trail (USFS 96B). Follow Chambers Lakes Trail about 2 miles. Where the trail opens out into a small clearing, turn right and follow a climbers' trail up a ridge next to an intermittent creek. About 30 minutes' hiking leads to timberline.

USFS 16, Three Creek Lake Road, and Park Meadow This route is sometimes used as an alternative approach to the north side of Broken Top. USFS 16 is not open in a normal snow year until late spring or early summer. From Sisters, turn south on Elm Street,.which quickly changes to USFS 16. Drive about 14 miles to the Park Meadow Trailhead. Hike about five miles west to Park Meadow. Leave the trail and hike up Park Creek to the north side of Broken Top.

Cascade Lakes Highway (Oregon 46) and Todd Lake Road (USFS 370). Use this route to approach Broken Top's crater. Cascade Lakes Highway and Todd Lake Road are generally open to Todd Lake by Memorial Day. From Bend, follow Cascade Lakes Highway almost 24 miles. Turn right on Todd Lake Road, USFS 370, and follow it less than half of a mile to the parking area for Todd Lake. Before the middle of July, the rest of USFS 370 is covered with snow and closed. Park at Todd Lake and hike or ski cross-country to Broken Top's crater.

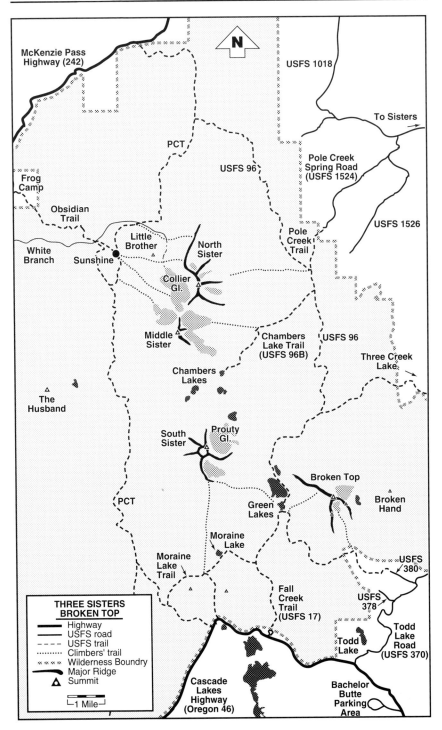

Cascade Lakes Highway (Oregon 46), Todd Lake Road (USFS 370), USFS 380, and Trail to Green Lakes. USFS 370 from Todd Lake north, and spur road 380 are not open until the snow has melted and the roadbed is dry. Sometimes this does not occur until August. When open, this route is the fastest approach to Broken Top's Northwest Ridge. The Trail to Green Lakes, which skirts around Broken Top, is slightly longer than Fall Creek Trail, but it starts 1,000 feet higher.

From Cascade Lakes Highway, follow Todd Lake Road almost four miles (avoid turning left at 3.3 miles on USFS 378). Turn left on USFS 380. The road is not marked with its number, but there is a sign that says "trailhead." Continue 1.3 miles on 380 and park where the road is blocked. Follow the abandoned road for one tenth of a mile to a sign marked Green Lakes. Follow this trail past an irrigation ditch, and continue west around Broken Top toward Green Lakes.

Cascade Lakes Highway (Oregon 46), Fall Creek Trail (USFS 17), and Green Lakes. Use this route to approach the east and north sides of South Sister and the Northwest Ridge of Broken Top. During a normal winter, huge snowdrifts form just east of Devils Lake. The Cascade Lakes Highway will not be opened until these drifts are cleared. Generally the road can be blasted through by Memorial Day. During exceptional years, the winds deposit so much snow that the road cannot be opened until July 4th. From Bend, follow Cascade Lakes Highway about 27 miles. Turn right at a sign for Green Lakes Trailhead. Hike about 4.7 miles to Green Lakes via Fall Creek Trail (USFS 17).

USFS SPECIAL AREA REGULATIONS

Besides general regulations which apply to all USFS wilderness areas in Oregon (see Introduction), the following additional restrictions apply to specific areas.

1. **Fire.** Building, maintaining, attending, or using a campfire is prohibited within the Sunshine and Obsidian area, within one-quarter mile of Husband or Eileen Lakes, within one-half mile of Camp Lake, Carver Lake, Moraine Lake, any of the four lakes known as Chambers Lakes, and any of the three lakes known as Green Lakes.
2. **Camping.** Camping is prohibited within 100 feet of Otter Lake, and Lower and Middle Erma Bell Lakes. Camping is also prohibited within 100 feet of all lakes, streams, ponds, springs, and trails within the Sunshine and Obsidian area, and the Linton Meadows, Husband Lake, and Eileen Lake areas.

THREE SISTERS MARATHON

Climbers have developed an unusual form of torture called the Three Sisters Marathon. The goal is to try and reach the summits of at least North Sister, Middle Sister, and South Sister in one twenty-four hour period. Traditionally the Marathon begins at Sunshine

The first Marathon took place on August 8, 1931, when Cliff Stalsberg, Ed Johnson, and Don Woods climbed the North, Middle, and South Sister in one day

(SS 12). At least two parties had tried a similar feat before. Emil Nordeen, Nels Skjersaa, Frank Haner, and Richard Guinee tried in 1926, and L.M. (Mace) Baldwin, Kent Shoemaker, and Frank J. Simpson tried in 1929. Both parties were unable to finish (Nordeen 1984; Annala 1976).

The game continues, but the ante has been steadily raised. Don Kohler, Lloyd Plaisted, and Jim Newsom added Little Brother on Aug. 31, 1952 (NS). Steve Schaefers and Gary Grimm added Broken Top in June 1970 (Kenyon 1970). The most recent record is a six-peak marathon, which includes Mt. Bachelor. This was first accomplished in 24 hours by Dale Moon and Ben Ross on July 18, 1970 with the aid of a car from the Broken Top roadhead to Mt. Bachelor (Kenyon 1970).

Gary Kirk, Gary Grimm, Steve Schaefers, and Dale Moon added a winter version of the Three Sisters Marathon in 1969. The Four Peaks Ski Mountaineering Expedition started from Bachelor Butte on day one and ended at the McKenzie Highway on day seven. The Expedition reached the summits of Broken Top, South Sister, and Middle Sister. The party was not able to complete the final 300 feet of North Sister (Kirk 1984).

NORTH SISTER DESCRIPTION (10,085')

North Sister is the most interesting climbing objective in the Three Sisters area because of a series of steep rock spires which line the summit ridge. From north to south the major spires are Glisan Pinnacle, Prouty Pinnacle, and the Camels Hump. Prouty Pinnacle forms the rough shape of a saddle with two horns on either end. The northern horn is the highest point on North Sister.

North Sister currently has four glaciers. Collier Glacier begins in the saddle at the base of the South Ridge and sweeps past the broad west face below the summit pinnacles. Linn Glacier is on the north face, Villard Glacier is on the northeast face, and Thayer Glacier is on the east face.

PROUTY PINNACLE VARIATIONS

Besides the regular route (see South Ridge description below), there are four other routes which lead to the top of Prouty Pinnacle.

When there is plenty of snow, the Northeast Shoulder is the most convenient way to gain Prouty Pinnacle from the north. Without snow, the climbing turns into a scary scramble up stacked dinner plates.

Gain the saddle between Glisan and Prouty Pinnacles. Move up the Northeast Shoulder of Prouty Pinnacle. Traverse left (south) onto a small snowfield. Follow the snowfield to the summit. The Northeast Shoulder was first climbed by Edwin T. Hodge, Alex C. Shipe, and Don Zimmerman, July 7, 1924 (NS; Hodge 1925).

Other routes up the summit pinnacle include the South Face, by Bill Byrd, Ray Harris, "Doc" Keller, and Eugene Sebring, May 27, 1951 (NS Obsidians); the southwest corner by Art Johnson, Silver (Norm) Lee, Anita Holmes, and Duane Brown, July 8, 1951 (NS Obsidians); and the rock rib on the left (north) side of the west-side chute. The rock on these three variations is quite poor.

North Sister summit pinnacles from the West   *Terry Toedtemeier photo*

NORTH SISTER DESCENT

To return to Pole Creek, descend the Southeast Ridge. To return to Sunshine descend the South Ridge. Climbers have used a gully below Glisan Pinnacle to descend the west face to Collier Glacier (see West Face Left). Do not use the gully if snow conditions are bad or the freezing level is high. Expect rockfall.

NORTH SISTER ROUTES

1 South Ridge

The South Ridge is the most popular way of climbing North Sister. You can approach the South Ridge from either Sunshine or Pole Creek. The crux of the climb is a traverse under the west face of Prouty Pinnacle. The slope is about 40 to 45 degrees and exposed. When icy, it can be quite formidable, especially to those not experienced in traversing. In late summer, the snowfield melts completely. Without snow, the slope is only 30 or 35 degrees, but insecure because of a covering of loose dirt and scree shaped like flat shingles.

The west-side chute, sometimes called the Bowling Alley, is a large amphitheater which leads from the north end of the traverse to the summit. It can be a fourth-class piece of cake when bare rock, or a verglased fifth-class nightmare. If there is any reason to suspect snow or ice on the upper reaches of the mountain, take crampons, helmet, and a rope. Take an ice ax, as you may find ice on the Collier early in the morning, and on shaded portions of the descent route.

From Sunshine, follow a climbers' trail southeast up Glacier Creek. Where the Creek turns south, continue southeast up the canyon toward the Collier Glacier. In summer, meadows gradually give way to scree and boulders, and the trail dissolves and reappears. Gain the western moraines of Collier Glacier just south of a prominent dark blade of rock at 8,200 feet, locally known as the Black Fin. Cross the glacier to the Southern tip of North Sister's South Ridge. Scramble up loose scree to the top of the ridge.

Follow the South Ridge, being careful not to tree yourself on several gendarmes in the first hundred yards. Near 9,800 feet, contour left around the west side of a large gendarme, sometimes called the Camels Hump. Move up, and wind around the east side of a second gendarme. Move back left again, and contour under the west face of a third gendarme to the base of the summit pinnacle.

Traverse 250 feet under the west face of Prouty Pinnacle. Turn right and climb into an obvious gully (The Bowling Alley) between the two horns of Prouty Pinnacle. Climb up and exit right near the top (fourth or fifth class, depending on conditions). You can also exit straight up, but this is a little harder. Move left and around the top of the Bowling Alley to the summit rim. Climb delightful rock to the top of the northern horn, which is the highest point.

The Bowling Alley is an obvious gully, yet many parties miss it and try to climb a more difficult gully off to the left. If you find yourself on a steep rotten wall, you

Middle and North Sister from the East   *Terry Toedtemeier photo*

have traversed too far north. Time from Sunshine and the PCT, 4-7 hours.

Variation 1A: Southeast Spur of South Ridge. The Southeast Spur is part of the South Ridge. Both routes share the crux traverse below the west side of Prouty Pinnacle and neither route has any technical climbing before they join at about 9,800 feet. The Southeast Spur is an alternative for reaching North Sister after approaching the mountain from the east via Pole Creek.

FR attempt of North Sister: George Woods and two others, Aug. 20, 1857. Some believe that Woods may have reached the summit of North Sister, but a close reading of his 1886 account shows that he did not (Woods 1886).

FRA of South Ridge and Prouty Pinnacle: Harley H. Prouty, August 9, 1910. H.H. Prouty also climbed Glisan Pinnacle and descended the Northwest Ridge in the same day (Prouty 1911).

FWA of South Ridge and North Sister, Robert L. Napier and Henry Noldan, Jan. 13, 1962 (NS; Napier 1962).

2 Thayer Glacier Headwall or East Face

Approach Thayer Glacier Headwall from Pole Creek. Pass the moraine on the bottom and climb up the center of a 40-to 45-degree face. Near the top, angle right (north) toward the saddle between Glisan and Prouty Pinnacle. Climb the northeast side of Prouty Pinnacle. Time from Pole Creek, 10-12 hours. Wear a helmet on the headwall because it forms a natural funnel for most of the rockfall on the east face. Avoid the Headwall after May unless the snowpack is high.

FRA: Bob Bauman and Leonard Woucik, June 19, 1965 (NS). Bauman found the route so straightforward and easy that he believed it must have been climbed prior to his ascent, but so far, no such record has been found (Bauman, Bob 1965).

3 East Buttress

Approach from Pole Creek Spring. Bypass the lower rock buttress to the north. Climb through a band of rotten rock via a gully. Sometimes the gully is iced-up, but usually it involves pitches of mixed snow, ice, and fifth-class rock. Steep (45 to 55 degree) snow slopes lead to a second rotten rock band. Pass through the barrier via a steep gully called Andesite Alley. The first ascent party encountered fifth-class climbing on rotten rock. After Andesite Alley, follow a ridge to Glisan Pinnacle. Climb the pinnacle directly, or pass around the left side. Finish up the Northeast Shoulder of Prouty Pinnacle. Time from timberline, 7-10 hours.

FA of Buttress, Nick Nicolai, Price Zimmermann, Ed Johann, Paul Kunkel, and Jim Snow, March 29, 1969 (Zimmermann 1969). They were unable to complete the final climb up Prouty Pinnacle. First complete ascent unknown.

4 Early Morning Couloir

As the name implies, you should be near the top of the couloir when day breaks, as it is a natural funnel for rockfall. Early Morning Couloir was named by the second ascent party, Nick Dodge and Gerald Calbaum (Dodge *Mazama* 1968).

Approach from Pole Creek Spring. Climb the couloir (maximum angle about 45 degrees). Near the top there are two choices. Go around the right side of the

North Sister from the Northeast   *Jim Hosmer photo*

headwall formed by Glisan Pinnacle, or climb the headwall directly. Reports vary as to the difficulty and the nature of the rock on the headwall. Some say the rock is good; others say it is marginal. Some say the climbing is consistent 5.7 or 5.8; others say the first moves are hard, but after that the climbing eases off to 5.1. Very likely it all depends on which section of the headwall you chose. One party climbed the headwall in full winter conditions. They reported extremely difficult climbing with little or no protection. From the top of Glisan Pinnacle, either climb the Northeast Shoulder of Prouty Pinnacle or descend and climb the regular west-side route. Time from timberline, 4-6 hours.

FA: Ted Davis, Ellen Thatcher, and Jan Newman, July 4, 1966. The summit register entry by Ted Davis reads, "Climbed gully posterior, south, of Villard Glacier." In a letter Davis stated that he could not remember exactly where they went when they reached Glisan Pinnacle, but he was certain they did climb the rock headwall (Davis 1984).

5 Villard Glacier

Villard Glacier is a straightforward and easy route; some might even call it a slog. Most parties move left onto the rib between Villard and Early Morning Couloir to avoid rockfall, which can be a serious problem. Near the top, skirt the west side of Glisan Pinnacle or climb its north face (possibly 5.7, see Early Morning Couloir). Climb either the northeast or west side of Prouty Pinnacle. The average angle of Villard is about 40 degrees. Climb only in early season. Approach from Pole Creek. Time from timberline, 4-7 hours.

FRA: Stan Hayden, John Lindstrom, and Phil Meany, June 22, 1958. They climbed the extreme right side of the glacier and bypassed Glisan Pinnacle. Lindstrom returned the following year, June 19, 1959, and soloed the left side of the glacier and the north wall of Glisan Pinnacle (NS; Lindstrom 1984).

6 Northeast Arete

The first ascent party approached from Sunshine, but the best approach is from Pole Creek Spring. Climb the Arete between Villard Glacier and Linn Glacier. From the top of the Arete, follow the Northwest Ridge to the summit. Time from timberline, 4-7 hours.

FA: Gary Leech and Hubert North, July 14, 1935 (NS). John Scott credited the first ascent of this route to Emil Nordeen, Nels Skjersaa, Frank Haner, and Richard Guinee on July 11, 1926 (Scott 1929). Scott based his statement on Nordeen's summit register entry. "Left Bend 1 a.m. reached here on summit at 7 a.m. Picked on the toughest–the east route" (NS).

In an interview, Emil Nordeen stated without hesitation that the only route he ever climbed on North Sister was the South Ridge. He said that "east route" meant that they had approached the mountain from eastern Oregon (Nordeen 1984).

7 Linn Glacier Headwall

The first ascent party climbed in August, but spring is a much better time. Approach from Pole Creek Spring or from Sunshine. The average angle of the

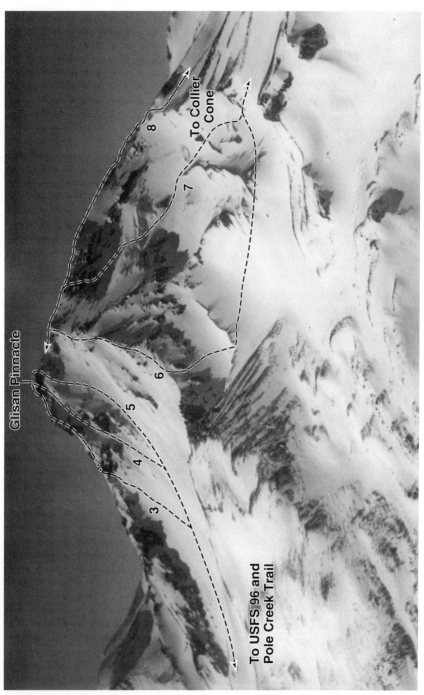

North Sister from the North

Jim Hosmer photo

route is about 40 degrees, but this is a poor gauge of its difficulty. The following description comes from the first ascent party's summit-register entry, and a member of that party's private journal.

> *Move out to the middle of the glacier and then head straight up it. At the base of the headwall a moat was crossed on a snow bridge. About 250 feet of rock climbing on the headwall (easy but rotten fifth-class) brought us into a snow couloir which we appropriately named 'shotgun alley'. We then climbed 550 feet up this couloir until the top of the north(west) ridge was gained. Bombarded by rocks constantly on wall. Hard hats saved us more than once.*(NS; Bauman, Tom 1981)

FA: Bill Robinson, Tom Bauman, and Bob Bauman, August 2, 1964.

8 Northwest Ridge

The Northwest Ridge is an easy route which can safely be climbed throughout the year. The crux of the route is climbing Prouty pinnacle.

Approach from either the PCT or from Sunshine. The first approach is longer but probably less tiring. Hike north and east on the PCT to Sawyer Bar. Do not follow the PCT across the lava flow, but continue east between Little Brother and Collier Cone. Cross beneath Collier Glacier, and gain the top of the Northwest Ridge around 7,500 feet.

The second approach is more direct but involves elevation loss and steeper ground. From Sunshine and the PCT, hike due east to a low saddle just south of Little Brother. Descend the moraine and cross just north of the snout of Collier Glacier. Slog up steep scree slopes to join the Ridge at about 9,000 feet.

Follow the ridge. Near the top, the ridge narrows, and several pinnacles seem to block further progress. Pass these obstacles by dropping slightly and traversing on the west side of the Ridge. Traverse south below Glisan Pinnacle. The traverse could be snow, ice, steep scree, or all three. From the col between Glisan and Prouty pinnacles, either climb the Northeast Shoulder of Prouty Pinnacle, or follow a ledge around northwest side of the pinnacle to the regular west-side route. Climb to the top. Time from Sunshine, 6-8 hours.

FRA of Northwest Ridge and Glisan Pinnacle: Louis F. Henderson, 1881 (King 1935). Henderson's decision to climb the Northwest Ridge was made spontaneously at timberline while he was botanizing. He was alone and without equipment of any kind. Just below Glisan Pinnacle he crossed a steep snowfield using the novel combination of running most of the way, then just before losing momentum and traction, lunging for the opposite side. Henderson did not climb Prouty Pinnacle. When he tried to reverse his run-and-gun maneuver while descending, he slipped and nearly slid down the west face of North Sister. Henderson felt that his near-death experience was a direct result of foolishness. He refrained from speaking of or writing about his climb for 51 years. Even now, few if any climbers know of his accomplishment (Henderson 1932; King 1935).

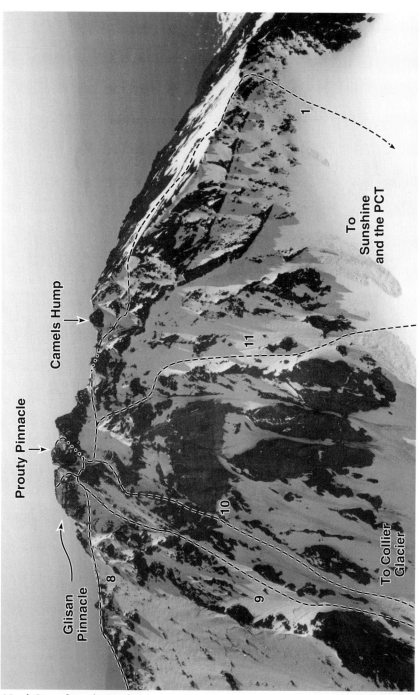

North Sister from the Southwest   *Terry Toedtemeier photo*

FD of Northwest Ridge from Prouty Pinnacle: Harley H. Prouty, Aug. 9, 1910 (Prouty 1911). After his first ascent of the true summit of North Sister, Prouty climbed Glisan Pinnacle and descended the Northwest Ridge, a feat just as difficult as the first complete ascent of the ridge 18 years later.

FA of Northwest Ridge and Prouty Pinnacle: John D. Scott, Perlee G. Payton, Wagar Carey Jr., and P. Gary Desiata, Aug. 8, 1929 (Scott 1929).

9 West Face Left

This route is steep enough to generate considerable rockfall, but not steep enough to be interesting. Its primary attraction is as a quick descent route from the west side of both Prouty and Glisan Pinnacle.

From Sunshine and the PCT, hike due east to a low saddle just south of Little Brother. Descend to Collier Glacier and cross to the base of the west face, directly below Glisan Pinnacle. Climb an obvious gully. Near the top, either climb straight up to the Glisan and Prouty Col, or veer right (south) to the Bowling Alley in the west face of Prouty. FA: unknown.

FD: Rodney Glisan, E.H. Loomis, July 20, 1903 (Glisan 1905).

10 West Face Direct

Approach from Sunshine. Start from Collier Glacier directly below Prouty Pinnacle. Climb up a couloir which cuts through the west-face cliffs. The couloir forks about 600 feet up, just after a narrow section in the first cliff band. Follow the left-hand fork 300 feet to a second fork. Again take the left-hand fork, which zigzags slightly, up to the base of the west-side snowfield below Prouty Pinnacle. Climb up the snowfield 300 feet and finish up the regular west-side route.

The average angle of the couloir is about 40 to 45 degrees. Rockfall is common in the narrow confines of the gully. Time from Sunshine, 4-6 hours.

FA: Bob Bauman, Ron Funke, and Tom Bauman, May 1, 1966.

11 West Face Right

The average angle of the climb is about 35 to 40 degrees. It is best done in early season to avoid rockfall. Approach from Sunshine.

FA: Ray Sims, Carl Knowles, Ed Johnson, and Eugene Pearson on Oct. 5, 1930. Ray Sims gives the following account of the climb.

> *The four roped together and with ice-axes ready, crossed Collier about the center. They experienced but one little 'thrill', that of the first three slipping and sliding down the 'glare-ice' a short distance, only to be stopped by their anchor man, Carl Knowles, who held the rope tight, while the others gained their footing. The foot of the mountain was finally reached, and the four climbers began the ascent straight up the Western side...It was harder climbing in this loose volcanic ash, but the 'Camel's hump' and the other narrow places were not encountered as the climbers came out right at the snow fields below Prouty Pinnacle. (Sims 1934)*

MIDDLE SISTER DESCRIPTION (10,047')

Middle Sister has a reputation for being an easy but dull mountain. It is not deserved. The west and north sides, although somewhat monotonous on the approach, soon achieve an alpine air that is missing from the south side of South Sister. And despite North Sister receiving all the accolades for difficulty, Middle Sister has several challenging routes on its steep eastern faces.

Middle Sister nurtures four glaciers, the Collier on the north, the Renfrew on the northwest, and the Hayden and Diller on the east.

MIDDLE SISTER ROUTES

12 North Ridge or Northwest Face

Middle Sister is most commonly climbed from the north or northwest. Both routes share the same approach, and present little in the way of climbing difficulty. The average gradient is less than 30 degrees, and there is no rock climbing.

The situation changes during bad weather. Like the South Side of Mt. Hood, the lack of definitive landmarks makes navigating the easy slopes of Middle Sister a nightmare in a whiteout. Take compass and map and know how to use them. Take an ice axe no matter what. If the freezing level is low, take crampons to cross Collier Glacier or Renfrew Glacier.

From Sunshine and the PCT, follow the PCT south to Sister Spring. Head east up a gully, south of a cliff band. Continue southeast to the lower end of Renfrew Glacier, staying just south of the odd-looking and aptly named "Dragons Back" rock formation. The tip of Renfrew Glacier may also be reached by following the climbers' trail up from Sunshine, then traversing south at about 7,000 feet to skirt around the Dragons Back. From this point, the shortest route to the summit takes a direct line up the Renfrew Glacier and the Northwest Face. Time from Sunshine, 3-5 hours.

A slightly longer route continues southeast from Sunshine toward the head of Collier Glacier. Once on the glacier, move southeast toward the north ridge of Prouty Peak, a small summit between North and Middle Sister. Find a narrow "V" slot through a small lava cone on the right side of Prouty Peak. Pass through this "V" to arrive at the Hayden and Renfrew Saddle at the foot of the North Ridge of Middle Sister. Follow the ridge to the summit. There is a short (150 feet), steep (50 degrees) section on the North Ridge which is insignificant when it is bare scree, but quite interesting for ill-equipped climbers early in the season. Time from timberline, 3-5 hours.

Some parties approach the North Ridge via Pole Creek Spring and Hayden Glacier. From timberline follow a ridge to the toe of Hayden Glacier. Ascend the glacier along the right side. There are plenty of crevasses on this small glacier, so rope up and watch out for thin snow bridges. Head for a saddle just north of Middle Sister, climb the moraine, and follow the north ridge to the top.

Three Sisters from the West   *USFS photo*

Middle Sister from the East

Terry Toedtemeier photo

FA: unknown. A party of seven men from Eugene visited Collier Glacier in August of 1860. The account of their travels implies that members of the party climbed Middle Sister on subsequent visits (McClung 1860). Professor Straub of the University of Oregon left a summit register on top of Middle Sister in 1892. According to the summit register, parties from Eugene reached the summit at least once a year in the 1890s.

FWA: possibly Jan. 1, 1926. A scrap of paper in Mazama archives contains the following entry.

> *Earliest climb of the year made on Jan. 1, 1926 by Ector Bossatti Mazama (Hank) Henry Cramer The Dalles.*

13 Southeast Ridge

Approach from Pole Creek Spring. Gain the ridge from the east via Diller Glacier, or from the south via Chambers Lakes, and follow it to the summit. Be careful on the lower ridge, as crevasses from Diller Glacier extend all the way to the lip of the ridge. Some skiers say that this is one of the best steep ski descents in the Three Sisters. **FA:** unknown.

14 East Face

Approach from Pole Creek Spring. Start at the bergschrund on Diller glacier and diagonal right 400 feet up a steep gully to a 20-foot rock wall. Climb the rock (5.1), then ascend the fall line to the summit. Climb in early season to avoid rockfall. Time from timberline, 5 hours.

FA: Jim Koontz and Jean Pierre Imhof on Aug. 19, 1954 (Koontz 1954).

15 East Arete

A good route. Approach from Pole Creek Spring and the medial moraine between Diller and Hayden Glacier. Follow the medial moraine to the base of the East Arete. Steep snow leads past an obvious pinnacle to the base of a rock band. Move slightly right, and rock climb just left of an obvious, wide couloir for 180 feet (easy fifth class). Climb a steep snowfield for 160 feet to a second rock band. Start up an obvious gully several feet to the right of the prow of the arete. After 40 feet, move right several feet (5.6), and climb up and left 40 feet to a ledge on the prow of the arete. Follow the snow-covered arete to the North Ridge. Follow the Ridge several-hundred feet to the summit. Time from timberline, unknown.

Variation 15A: You can avoid the rock climbing difficulties of the lower rock bands by starting further south on Diller Glacier and climbing up and right, threading your way through two short rock bands to gain the upper arete.

FA: Tom Bauman and Ken Jern, April 27, 1968 (Bauman, Tom 1981).

FA of Variation 15A: Nick Dodge, Jim O'Connell, Nick Nicolai, and Price Zimmermann, June 15, 1969 (MS).

16 Northeast Face Direct

Approach from Pole Creek Spring. Hike up to the head of Hayden Glacier. Start below a prominent couloir in the northeast face just left of a large 500-foot-high rock buttress. Cross the main bergschrund and a smaller bergschrund higher up, and climb to the base of a 50-foot rock band. In winter or early spring a waterfall will sometimes cover all or part of the rock band. Climb the waterfall. If the waterfall is not in condition, climb the rock band (technically easy fifth-class climbing, but rotten).

Climb another 100 feet up lower-angle mixed ground. Continue up 50-degree snow for about 300 feet. Either continue up the couloir to the North Ridge, or angle up and left to the East Arete and follow it to the North Ridge. Follow the North Ridge to the summit. Time from timberline, 5-7 hours.

FA: Bob Bauman, Ron Funke, and Tom Bauman, May 1, 1966. Later in the day they continued on to North Sister and were able to complete a new line up the center of the West Face (MS).

SOUTH SISTER DESCRIPTION (10,358')

South Sister is the third highest peak in Oregon, with the highest lake in Oregon contained in its almost perfect summit crater. Hodge (1925) has a superb description of the mountain.

> *The South Sister is the youngest of the Three Sisters. It, however, is not a unified peak, but is a comparatively young mountain built upon and around the wrecked remains of an ancient Elder South Sister. Neither of these South Sisters are comparable in great age to the North Sister. If it were possible to rename these peaks at the present time, the North Sister should be called the Mother, and the Middle and South Sisters Daughters. The South Sister, by reason of its youth, is the most symmetrical mountain in the group. The Elder South Sister, which protrudes through its eastern slope, disfigures its almost perfect shape. Here we see that a mountain, like a human being, contains within itself part of its ancestors.*

Since the last ice age, South Sister has produced several pumice and obsidian flows on its south and east sides. The mountain could still be active, but there is no record of any activity since European settlements have been near the mountain.

South Sister has quite a number of permanent snowfields and several glaciers, the most important of which is Prouty Glacier on the northeast side. The north side was extensively altered by glaciation in the past, but the current Skinner and Eugene glaciers are much too small to be of any consequence in the process now.

SOUTH SISTER ROUTES

17 South Side via Green Lakes or Devils Lake

The South Side is the easiest and most accessible route in this book, but if there is snow on the route, you must have crampons and ice axe. Once the snow melts, usually by mid to late July, specialized equipment is not needed. Use the route from Devils Lake if you are trying to climb South Sister and return to the car in one day. You may also climb via Green Lakes in one day, but the route is longer and takes more time. An increasing number of climbers are attempting the South Side in winter or spring and descending on skis.

To climb South Sister in one day, drive about 29 miles from Bend on the Cascade Lakes Highway. Turn left and park in Devils Lake Campground. Follow the South Sister Climbers' Trail north across the highway and up a steep draw between Devils Hill and Kaleetan Butte. The trail leaves the woods after 1.5 miles and intersects a second trail. Moraine Lake is to the right (east), and Wickiup Plain is to the left (west). Ignore both and proceed north across a sparsely wooded plateau. About three miles from the trailhead, the trail deteriorates. Follow one of many trails toward the summit. Near 8,900 feet, intersect the terminal moraine of the Lewis Glacier and the climbers' trail from Green Lakes. Skirt Lewis Glacier on the left and follow the scree slope to the crater rim. Continue around the eastern rim to the true summit on the northeast side. Time from Devils Lake, 5-8 hours.

From Green Lakes follow the western fork of Fall Creek up a small canyon on the north edge of Newberry Lava Flow. Continue up the canyon to the southern edge of Lewis glacier. Skirt the glacier to the south, and join the Devils Lake climbers' trail. Time from Green Lakes, 3-5 hours.

During the climb, avoid leaving the safety of the scree for the apparent ease of the Lewis Glacier unless you are equipped with crampons, ice axe, and rope.

FA: unknown. The unpublished diary of Adolph Dekum indicates that the summit of South Sister might have been used for religious purposes by Indians. Adolph Dekum noted stacks of rock on the summit, some of them five to six feet high. He found similar rock structures on Bachelor Butte, Maiden Peak, and Bald Peter (Dekum 1883). The rock piles described by Dekum may have been left over from what anthropologist call a vision quest.

> *Power is sought from a host of spirits whose characteristics are not sharply defined. These are predominantly birds and animals, winds, lightning and the like...There are times that are especially propitious; at puberty, in distress, or on the loss of a wife, a husband, or a child. The mode of seeking and the revelation are stereotyped: one fasts at night on mountain tops, running about, piling up rocks.* (Spier 1930)

Since the vision quest was characteristic of most if not all Northwest Indian

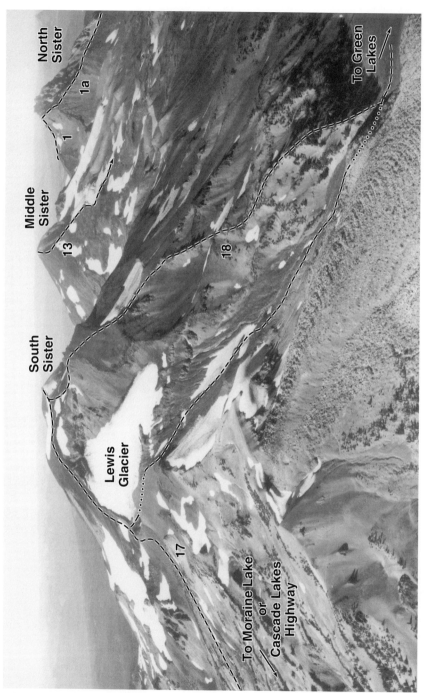

Three Sisters from the Southeast

Leonard Delano photo

tribes, it is impossible to say which tribe was responsible for the structures.

18 Old Crater

Old Crater follows the southeast ridge of South Sister, which is actually part of an older parent volcano (see Description at the beginning of this chapter). Although the ridge probably was never part of a crater, the name has stuck.

Hike west from Green Lakes. Follow one of two moraines which lead to the southeast ridge. The top of the ridge is fairly broken up. Try to avoid treeing yourself by skirting low on the south side. Climb up to the crater rim. The highest point is to the right on the northeast rim. Time from Green Lakes, 5-7 hours.

FRA: Judge John Waldo, Adolph Dekum, and Edward Humason, Sept. 12, 1883 (Dekum 1883).

19 Prouty Glacier

Approach from Green Lakes. Hike north from the northwest end of Green Lakes basin for about one-half mile. Turn west and hike up a prominent gully to Prouty Glacier at the base of the northeast face. Climb up Prouty glacier to the southern bergschrund and just below an obvious couloir. Follow the couloir through the rock bands. Near the top, gain the summit ridge, west of the low point between the false and true summits. Climb to the crater rim. The highest point is to the right on the northeast rim.

FRA: Gary Leech and Hubert North, July 17, 1935. Leech is not clear in his Mazama summit register entry about which route he climbed, but his entry in the Obsidian register is clear (SS, Obsidian).

20 Prouty Headwall

There are at least two routes on the cliffs above Prouty Glacier. On August 26, 1959 Jerry Ramsey, Jim Ramsey, and Jack Watts climbed several pitches of easy fifth-class rock to the right of Prouty Glacier Route (Ramsey 1984). John Lindstrom, Brad Reed, and Robert Napier climbed the second route through Prouty Headwall on July 25, 1965 (SS). It follows a semi-hidden couloir through the center of the headwall. Rockfall is common on both routes. Avoid the Headwall after June. The summit registers hint that several parties blundered up this headwall while trying to find other routes. During recent interviews, they could not recall where they went.

21 North Ridge

The North Ridge is the best route for parties wishing to approach South Sister from the north, including climbers trying to complete a Sisters Marathon.

Most of the North Ridge is a grunt up a typical volcanic ridge. The crux of the climb is moving around the right (west) side of a large rock buttress at about 9,800 feet. Above the buttress, follow the lower-angle slope to the summit.

FRA: Don Woods, Cliff Stalsberg, and Ed Johnson, Aug. 8, 1931 (SS). Another party may have climbed the North Ridge before 1931. Earl A. Britton wrote the following comment seven days after Woods, Stalsberg, and Johnson made their

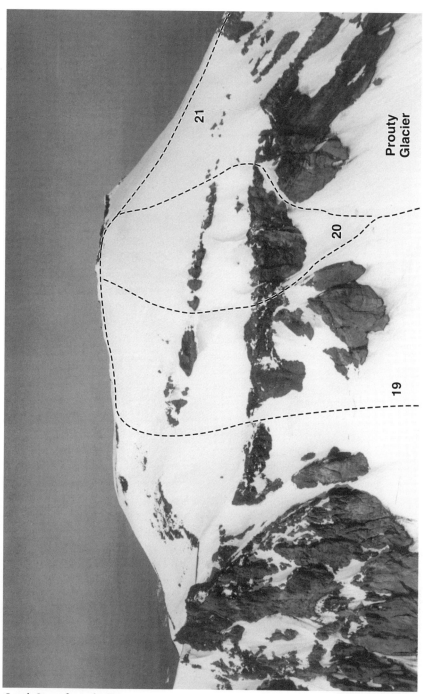

South Sister from the East

Terry Toedtemeier photo

South Sister from the North   *Terry Toedtemeier photo*

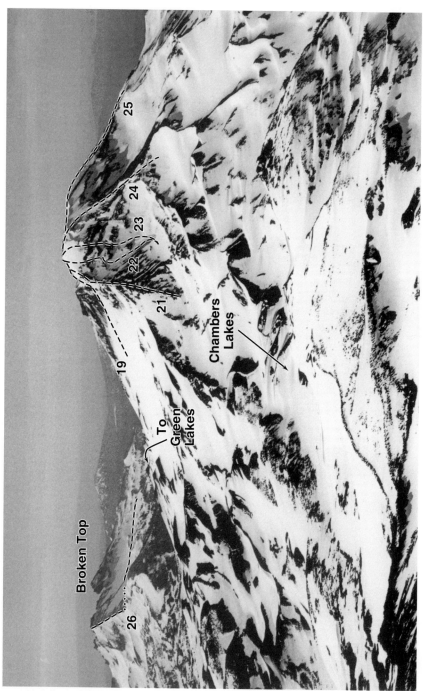

South Sister from the North

Terry Toedtemeier photo

climb. "Hello-Stalsberg-Woods-Johnson-you are all wet. I brought a party from Roseberg up on north side of this mountain" (SS).

It is unclear whether Britton is saying that he did the first ascent, or whether he is stating that the climb is easy. Britton left a diary of his climbs. It does not always note how he climbed South Sister, but the approaches he used indicate that his ascents on the north side were probably up the Northwest Ridge (Britton 1931).

22 Silver Couloir

Silver Couloir is a straightforward, 45-degree snow slope between the North Ridge and the North Face Couloir. Climb early in the season and early in the morning to avoid rockfall. Vertical waterfalls sometimes form to the right of the route on the upper rockband. Approach from Green Lakes.

FRA: Gerald Calbaum, Nick Dodge, and Gary Kirk, 1973 (Dodge 1975).

23 North Face Couloir

The North Face Couloir is in a true north-facing cirque like Eliot Headwall on Mt. Hood. Usually the North Face Couloir is a snow climb, but during the right conditions, you will find multiple pitches of ice. Unfortunately the base of the climb is a long distance from any trailhead, especially in winter and spring.

Approach from Pole Creek Spring or Green Lakes. Follow the prominent couloir on the north face which splits three separate rock bands. The couloir pinches down through the last rock band, and you must climb two steep pitches to exit onto the summit slopes above. Climb early in the season and early in the morning to avoid rockfall.

FRA: Jim Blanchard and two others whose names were not recorded, July 19, 1967 (Blanchard 1990). Jim Blanchard said that he tried this route on a recommendation, and that someone had climbed the route before his ascent.

24 Northwest Ridge

You can approached this climb from Pole Creek, Green Lakes, or Obsidian Trail and Linton Meadows. The Northwest Ridge has no technical climbing, but it is a long grind from all three trailheads. **FA:** unknown.

25 West Ridge

Approach the West Ridge from Obsidian Trail and Linton Meadows. The West Ridge is easy, but it is a long grind from Frog Camp. **FA:** unknown.

BROKEN TOP DESCRIPTION (9,175')

Broken Top, like its more famous cousin to the north, Mt. St. Helens, forms a very rough horseshoe. The similarity ends there. Mt. St. Helens is a young volcano whose shape is the result of a massive explosion. Broken Top is a very old volcano whose shape is the result of implosion and the subsequent collapse of the summit. Despite its geologic age, Broken Top looks surprisingly young. Geologists theorize that the mountain is still standing because of its position east of the Cascade crest.

With less snowfall, there has been correspondingly less erosion over the years.

All of the south side and much of the interior of Broken Top is gone. With the inside so easily visible, it is one of the better examples of how volcanos build themselves with alternating layers of pumice, ash, and lava flow. There are two glaciers on Broken Top, the Crook glacier within the crater, and the Bend glacier on the north side.

BROKEN TOP DESCENT

The only recommended descent in summer and late fall is down the Northwest Ridge or the scree slopes of the west face (see route description below).

The best descent in winter or spring is a traverse south along the base of the rock forming the west crater rim, to the top of Eleven O'Clock Couloir. Downclimb the 50-degree gully for 500 feet, and walk south out of the crater to Dutchman Flat Sno-Park or Todd Lake. If Eleven O'Clock Couloir looks dangerous or too steep, continue down to Nine O'Clock Couloir and descend it. Under no conditions should you descend the couloirs when they are bare of snow.

BROKEN TOP ROUTES

26 Northwest Ridge

The Northwest Ridge is the most popular climb on Broken Top because it is technically easy and the rock is solid when it has to be. Approach from Green Lakes, or USFS 370 and 380.

From Green Lakes, hike due east and follow a trail which leads to a saddle on the Northwest Ridge just below 8,000 feet.

Use USFS 370, USFS 380, and the trail to Green Lakes which skirts around the south side of Broken Top, if you are looking for the fastest approach to Broken Top's Northwest Ridge. The trail is slightly longer than Fall Creek Trail, but it starts 1,000 feet higher. USFS 370 and 380 are not opened until the snow has melted and the roadbed is dry. Sometimes this does not occur until August.

From the saddle in the Northwest Ridge, follow the trail up the ridge to the northwest corner of a 15-foot rock band. Climb a large crack in good rock just left of the northwest corner, or a dirty groove about 20 feet south of the northwest corner. The climbing is short and easy (fourth class or 5.1), but some may prefer the security of a rope.

Move up and right over a terraced scree-and-boulder field to a vertical wall that forms the base of the summit pinnacle. Follow a sloping ramp south along the wall. The ramp rises gradually, and the wall shrinks in height. About 60 feet south, turn the south side of the vertical wall, which is now little more than six feet high. Follow the ramp north and scramble up horrible rock to the summit. Time from Green Lakes, 2-4 hours.

Variation 26A. A layer of hard rock caps the northern end of the summit of Broken Top. It also forms a ridge on the northwest corner of the summit pinnacle,

Broken Top from the Northwest   *Jim Hosmer photo*

which provides a delightful 50 feet of easy fifth class (5.2) climbing with just the right amount of exposure.

FRA: Thomas Eliot, Harley Prouty, and Charles Whittlesey, Aug. 15, 1910. They wrote:

> *Undersigned started from Camp Riddell 9 am Aug. 13, crost the divide between the Middle and South Sister, arriving at small lake at foot of the red side of the N.W. Ridge of Broken Top at 5 pm. Starting at 5 am Sunday, we climbed to the base of the mountain at 8 am and to the summit at 9:30 am finding no previous record of ascent. We came up little chimney immediately below and to the northeast of the top, Prouty coming alone a little to the left (as you come up), just below top of the red thumb to N.E., and tying rope for the others to pull themselves up. We consider going down by red ledge to the south by west, then back to the right (north) zigzagging. (BT)*

27 Nine-O'Clock Couloir (First Notch)

The names Nine O'Clock Couloir and Eleven O'Clock Couloir were coined by John Chunn of Bend, Oregon as an easy way to distinguish two similar couloirs. If you are standing inside the crater with the summit oriented at twelve o'clock, one couloir is at nine o'clock and the other at eleven o'clock.

From inside of Broken Top's Crater, climb toward the lowest point in the crater wall between the main summit and the southwest summit. After passing the bergschrund, climb about 150 feet up a narrow 45-degree gully to the crater rim. Move north below the west crater rim to the notch where Eleven O'Clock Couloir ends. Continue north under the cliffs of the crater rim, to the point where the Northwest Ridge meets the summit pinnacle.

The slope traversed from Eleven O'Clock Couloir to the Northwest Ridge is about 40 degrees when there is snow or ice. In the summer, the traverse alternates between steep scree and a rough trail right up against the rock. Climb the summit pinnacle. Do not attempt Nine O'Clock Couloir after the snow melts out of the upper gully, generally in late July. Time from Crater, 2-3 hours.

FA: unknown.

28 Eleven-O'Clock Couloir (Second Notch)

From inside of Broken Top's crater, climb into a narrow gully between the low point in the southwest crater wall (Nine-O'Clock Couloir), and the summit pinnacle. The gully is about 500 feet and averages about 50 degrees. A cornice can form at the top, and the last 10 feet to the base of the cornice can approach vertical.

Once at the top of the couloir, it is tempting to continue up the crater rim. Do not be tempted. The rim leads to a rotten headwall. The headwall has all the stability of compacted graham crackers.

Broken Top from the South   *John Lindstrom photo*

Continue north under the cliffs of the crater rim to the point where the Northwest Ridge meets the summit pinnacle. The slope is about 40 degrees when there is snow or ice. In the summer, the going alternates between loose scree and a rough trail right up against the rock. Climb the summit pinnacle. Do not climb Eleven O'Clock Couloir after the snow melts out of the upper gully, generally in late July. Time from Crater, 2-3 hours.

FA: unknown.

29 High Noon (Direct Crater Wall)

From inside Broken Top's crater, start climbing directly beneath the summit in a gully. Follow the fall line up and slightly right. Traverse left across a snowfield when high enough to gain a left-treading snow ramp. Follow the snow ramp up and left, then climb four or five pitches of steep (60 degree) snow and or ice to the summit. Depending on conditions, you may have to cross an occasional rock band. Bring protection to set up belays on the rock. The angle of the last pitch to the top varies depending on the route you chose. A direct line to the summit stays on 60-degree ground. Moving off left leads to gentler ground sooner.

Timing is all-important when planning an ascent of this face, to minimize climbing on the miserable rock. The inside of the crater acts like a giant reflector oven and snow quickly melts from the crater wall. The key is to hit the climb just after a freeze and thaw cycle, which generally only occurs in winter or late spring. Ice screws, pickets, and rock protection may be necessary, although hard to place, as the snow and ice is usually shallow. Time from crater, 2-4 hours.

FRA: Jack Barrar and John Richmond, June 27, 1970. Barrar made the following comment in the summit register. "First ascent of ice gully directly up east face (not 1st notch, not 2nd notch, but crater wall). No shit, it was hairer than hell!" (BT).

30 South Face Gully

You can climb this route with or without snow.

Start in Broken Top's crater. Slog northeast up a low-angle face to a low point in the summit ridge between the northwest summit and the northeast summit. Follow the crater rim west to the summit pinnacle. The rim varies in thickness and the rock varies in quality. You will probably encounter some fourth-or easy fifth-class climbing. Climb two short and easy, but crumbly, walls to the summit. Time from Crater, 1-2 hours.

FRA: Armin Furrer, Leo Harryman, Stuart Rae, Phil Philbrook, and Ervin McNeal, Aug. 5, 1923. Broken Top was the second mountain "The Boys from Bend" climbed in 1923. They would go on to claim the first ascents of Mt. Washington and Three Fingered Jack. Their route up the crater wall was probably a first ascent. Two separate contemporary accounts give a good idea where the Boys from Bend climbed. "Climbed barehanded by ridge on N.E. Consider descending by Mazama Route" (BT). "Five Bend youths...made the dangerous climb up Broken Top from inside the crater" (*Central Oregon Press* 1923).

31 Northeast Spur

After climbing the Northeast Spur, Nick Dodge wrote, "We are sure what we climbed was buried last year and will be gone next year" (BT). The first ascent party was more blunt, saying that the rock was "extremely rotten" and that the route was "not recommended" (BT).

FA: Bob Ashworth, Bob Bauman, Charles Eubanks, Mike Gilbert, and Jim Harrang, Aug. 25, 1962 (BT).

32 North Face

Like the other routes on the north face of Broken Top, the rock on the North Face is extremely rotten. During the first ascent, one member of the party had his helmet cracked when it sustained a direct hit from falling debris. Climb only in winter or early spring. Approach from Three Creek Lake in late spring or early summer or from Bachelor Butte in winter.

FA: Steve Recken, George Selfridge, and Dennis Stephens, Aug. 28, 1966.

33 North Face Couloir

The first ascent party climbed the North Face Couloir in August. They wrote: "Straight up Bend Glacier, across mud and scree slopes into snow gully to summit. Crampons will ball in mud too!" (BT).

You will find this route safer and more interesting in early season when the "mud and scree" is covered by snow. In winter, approach the north side from Bachelor Butte via the unnamed moraine lake between Broken Hand and the southeast summit of Broken Top. Cross a natural pass just northwest of the lake which leads to the Bend Glacier.

FA: John Lindstrom and Herb Merker, Aug. 30, 1964.

34 North Buttress

The North Buttress can only be climbed in winter under cold conditions. Approach from Bachelor Butte via the unnamed moraine lake between Broken Hand and the southeast summit of Broken Top. Cross a natural pass just northwest of the lake which leads to the Bend Glacier.

Cross to the far-western side of the Bend Glacier and enter a gully which ends just below the Northwest Snowfield. Climb two to three rope-lengths up the gully (average angle about 45 degrees). Exit up a ramp on the right just below a mini-amphitheater. Climb one five-to 10-foot vertical section of ice. From the top of the ramp, climb straight up a 45-degree snowfield to the summit pinnacle. Move to the northeast side of the pinnacle, and follow a snowslope to the summit. Take pickets and one or two ice screws.

FRA: John Chunn and David Schermer, Dec. 18, 1988 (Schermer 1989).

Summit Pinnacle of Mt. Thielsen   *Peter Green photo*

MT. THIELSEN (9,182')

Climbed to the top of ...Mt. Tiesen (Thielsen) today. Note:
in ascending a difficult peak, mark well how to get down.
John B. Waldo on climbing the summit pinnacle in 1886

DESCRIPTION

Mt. Thielsen is the seventh-highest peak in Oregon. It is characterized by a remarkable summit pinnacle. From some angles, the pinnacle looks so slender and sharp that climbing, much less standing on the summit, would be impossible. Because of the height and prominence of the pinnacle, it is often struck by lightning, and has been nicknamed the Lightning Rod of the Cascades.

Mt. Thielsen is thought to be similar in age and origin to Mt. Washington and Three Fingered Jack. All three mountains formed during a period of Cascade volcanism that ended before the last ice age 100,000 years ago. Glaciation and other forms of erosion have significantly reduced each mountain, and in the case of Mt. Washington and Mt. Thielsen, exposed interior plugs of basaltic andesite. The 80-foot summit pinnacle of Mt. Thielsen is part of the andesite plug. It has excellent rock. Rock quality on the rest of the mountain is generally poor.

MAPS

The following maps are currently (1991) available for Mt. Thielsen.
1. Diamond Lake, 7.5 minute quadrangle, published by USGS in 1985.
2. Mt. Thielsen, 7.5 minute quadrangle, published by USGS in 1985.
3. Rogue-Umpqua Divide, Boulder Creek, and Mt. Thielsen Wilderness, published by the USFS, date unknown.

ROUTES

1 Regular Route

Drive to Diamond Lake on State Highway 138. Park in a paved trailhead on the east side of Highway 138, and follow the Mt. Thielsen Trail (USFS 1456) four miles to a junction with the PCT. Cross the PCT and continue east up the west ridge of Thielsen, following a climbers' trail. When you reach timberline, either continue up the west ridge (third-or fourth-class), or cut south, and then east up scree and boulder fields. Both routes eventually lead to a notch on the south ridge, just below the summit pinnacle. Move around to the east side of the pinnacle and scramble up 80 feet of easy rock climbing (5.1). The summit is small, but will accommodate four to six people without forcing undue intimacy. Time from trailhead, 3-5 hours.

FA: Ensign E.E. Hayden, Summer 1883 (Diller 1884). Hayden was a part of a U.S. Geological Survey party which made a detailed inspection of the Southern Oregon Cascades in the summer of 1883. Hayden collected samples of fulgurite on the summit for J.S. Diller, who later wrote an article about them. If not for Diller's article, Hayden's climb would have gone unrecorded. Judge John Waldo repeated Hayden's climb in 1886 (Waldo 1880-1907), as did Harley H. Prouty and Eugene Compher in the Fall of 1910. Prouty thought he was doing a first ascent, but found records of several other parties on the summit (Prouty 1916).

2 McLaughlin Memorial (III-5.7)

Most of the rock on this climb is solid, but according to the first ascent party there are two sections of horrible rock which cannot be protected. The route honors Mark McLaughlin of Eugene. He died on Mt. Mckinley in 1967, when he and his party were trapped by a ferocious storm near the summit.

Drive to Diamond Lake on State Highway 138. At the north end of Diamond Lake, turn west and follow signs to Diamond Lake Resort. Just after the road curves south, turn left into a parking area for Howlock Mt.Trail (USFS 1448). Follow Howlock Mt. Trail about 3.5 miles to where it divides. Turn right and follow Thielsen Creek Trail (USFS 1449) about 3.5 miles to the PCT. Cross the PCT and continue south up Thielsen Creek to the base of Lathrop Glacier.

1. Start on the east side of Lathrop Glacier at the base of the Northeast Buttress. Scramble 200 feet up easy slabs.
2. Climb up right-facing dihedrals for 150 feet (5.6). Belay below a gully.
3. Climb to the end of the gully. Climb a crack (5.6) 75 feet to a small ledge.
4. Move up and right for 75 feet. Move left and up on slabs to a large ledge.
5. Scramble up easy ground for 75 feet. Traverse 75 feet left to a belay ledge.
6. Climb up and left onto the prow of the Northeast Buttress. Follow the buttress 20 feet, then traverse back 50 feet and climb up to a belay ledge.
7. 8. & 9. Climb 75 feet up and right to a lower-angle area which holds snow until late summer. Easy scrambling leads up for several pitches.
10. About 150 feet of fourth class on the buttress leads to a good belay.
11. Traverse left and climb a steep knobby wall (5.6 on unstable rock) for 40 feet. Climb up and left into a large gully.
12. & 13. Follow the low-angle but rotten gully to the regular route. Time from Diamond Lake, 8-10 hours.

FA: Bob Bauman, Tom Bauman, and Gary Kirk, Sept. 26, 1968 (Kirk 1984).

BIBLIOGRAPHY

Annala, Eino E. 1976. *The Crag Rats.* Hood River, Oregon: Hood River News.
Bauman, Bob. 1965. Letter to Nick Dodge, 9 Dec. 1965. Courtesy of Nick Dodge.
———. 1986. Interview with author, 5 Aug. 1986.
Bauman, Tom. 1981. Interview with author, taped 2 Dec.1981.
———. 1986. Letter to author, 18 June 1986.
Beckey, Fred. 1960. Mount Hood Yocum Ridge. *American Alpine Club Journal:* 122-124.
Bend Bulletin. 1923. Final Peak is Conquered by Bend Climbers, 4 Sept. 1923. Courtesy of Phil Philbrook.
Biewener, John. 1956. A Climber's Guide to Mt. Hood. *Mazama.*
Blanchard. Jim. 1990. Telephone conversation with author, 30 Oct. 1990.
Blanchard, Smoke. 1985. *Walking Up and Down in the World.* San Francisco: Sierra Club Books.
Blust, Tom. 1988. Letter to author, 1988.
Britton, Earl A. 1931. Unpublished diary. Courtesy of Mrs. Earl A. Britton.
Broken Top summit register. 1911-1969. Mazama Library.
Brunk, George. 1984. Letter to author, 26 June 1984.
Callis, Pat. 1986. Telephone conversation with author.
Central Oregon Press. 1923. Bend Boys Second to Reach Summit of Broken Top. Courtesy Phil Philbrook.
Chisholm, Colin. 1981. Interview with author, 4 Aug. 1981.
Combs, Al. 1985. Letter to author, 31 Jan. 1985.
Corruccini, R.J. (Joe). 1986. Letter to author, 18 May 1986.
Crandell, Dwight R. 1980. Recent Eruptive History of Mt. Hood. *USGS Bulletin 1492.*
Cummins, William S. 1964. New Routes on Three Fingered Jack. *Mazama.*
Darr, Everett. 1932. The Wy'east Trail. Unpublished manuscript. Courtesy Wy'east Club.
———. 1937. 1937 Mazama Mountaineering Review. *Mazama.*
———. 1936. Wy'east Mountaineering. *The Wy'east Climber.* 19-21.
———. 1970. Telephone conversation with Don Hall, 29 June 1970, courtesy of Don Hall.
Davis, Ted. 1984. Letter to author, 19 Nov. 1984.
Dekum, Adolph. 1883. Unpublished diary of 1883 trip through the Cascades with Judge Waldo. Courtesy of Francesca Dekum Mills.
Dierdorff, James G. 1857. Ascension of Mt. Hood. *Democratic Standard,* 27 Aug. 1857. Courtesy of Mazama Library.
Diller, J.S. 1884. Fulgurite from Mount Thielsen, Oregon. *American Journal of Science,* 3d ser. 28: 252-258.

Bibliography

Doane, O.D. 1872. An Ascent of Mount Hood. *The Weekly Mountaineer*, 11 Aug. 1872. Courtesy of Mazama Library.

Dodge, Nicholas A. 1968. North Sister's East Face. *Mazama.*

——. 1968. *A Climber's Guide to Oregon.* Portland: Mazamas.

——. 1975. *A Climbing Guide to Oregon.* Beaverton: Touchstone Press.

——. 1985. Interview with author, 18 Dec. 1985.

Dryer, T.J. 1854. First Ascent of Mt. Hood. *Oregonian,* 19 Aug. 1854.

Evening Telegram. 1901. Portlanders on Jefferson, 16 Aug. 1901. Courtesy of Mazama Library.

Forest Service, U.S. 1990. Environmental Assessment Wilderness Strategies Project.

Gibbons, Tom. 1957. Mt. Washington by the East Face. *Mazama.*

Grauer, Jack. 1975. *Mt. Hood: A Complete History.* Portland.

Hackett, Bill. Interview with author, 29 July 1981.

Hall, Don Alan. 1975. *On Top of Oregon.* Corvallis: Golden West Press.

Harrang, Jim. 1985. Interview with author.

Harris, Stephen L. 1976. *Fire and Ice.* Seattle: The Mountaineers, Pacific Search Press.

Hatch, Laura. 1917. The Glaciers of Mt. Jefferson. *Mazama.*

Henderson, Professor Louis F. 1932. Early Experiences of a botanist in the Northwest. Talk before the Oregon Audubon Society. Oregon Historical Society. Microfilm #112.

Hitchcock, Dave. 1988. Interview with author.

Hodge, Edwin T. 1925. *Mount Multnomah.* Eugene: University of Oregon.

Hood River News. 1928. Unusual Ascent of Hood is Made, 31 Aug. 1928.

Illumination Rock summit register. 1911-1952. Mazama Library.

Johnson, V.E. 1931. Letter to Donald G. Onthank, 16 Sept., 1931. Courtesy of Mrs. D.G. Onthank.

Journal. 1907. Mazama Members Due in Portland Tomorrow, 28 July 1907. Courtesy of Mazama Library.

——. 1934. Jefferson Park Landslide, 19 Oct. 1934.

Kenyon, Ed. 1970. Eugeneans Claim Climbing Record. *Eugene Register Guard,* 21 July 1970.

King, Clarence. 1871. On the Discovery of Actual Glaciers on the Mts of the Pacific Slope. *American Journal of Science,* 3d ser. 1 (Jan.-June): 157-167.

King, Sid. 1935. Henderson Tells About First Ascent of North Sister. *Eugene Register Guard,* 6 Aug. 1935. Bx 196:9, Obsidian Records, Inc., Special Collections, Knight Library, University of Oregon.

Kirk, Gary. 1984. Telephone conversation with author.

Koontz, Jim. 1954. Middle Sister. *Basecamp* 62.

——. 1955. Mountaineering. *Western Outdoor Quarterly,* May 1955, 6.

Langille, William A. 1937. Ax 235, Langille Papers. Special Collections, Knight Library, University of Oregon.

Lawrence, Donald B. 1958. Glaciers and Vegetation in Southeastern Alaska. *American Scientist* 46 (June):89-94.

Lee, Greg. 1984. Hood Trail Record Set. *Oregonian*, 9 Sept. 1984.

Leech, Gary. 1933. Unpublished manuscripts. Courtesy of Smoke Blanchard Estate.

——1954. Illumination Rock. *Mazama*.

Lewis, Hank. 1986. Interview with author, 13 March 1986.

Lindstrom, John. 1984. Letters to author 24 Nov. 1984, 15 Dec 1984 & 19 March 1989.

Lizee, Phil. 1984. Letter to author, 23 Nov. 1984.

——. 1964. Mt. Jefferson. *Cascadians 1964 Annual.*

Margosian, Leon. 1947. Mt. Washington via the West Ridge. *Mazama*.

Massey, E.L. 1854. A Trip to Mt. Jefferson. *The Oregon Statesman*, 22 Aug. 1854.

Mazama. 1905. A Forbidding Day on Mt. Jefferson.

——. 1907. The First Ascent of Mt. Jefferson.

——. 1940. Up the South Face of Mt. Washington, under Mountaineering Notes.

Mazamas. 1907. Prospectus on the Fourteenth Annual Outing. Courtesy Mazama Library.

McArthur, Lewis A. 1982. *Oregon Geographic Names*. 5th ed. Portland:Western Imprints.

McClung, J.H. 1860. Recollections of a Trip up the McKenzie River in the Fall of 1860. Unpublished manuscript. Courtesy of Gerald W. Williams.

McJury, Russ. 1936. Ascent of North Face of Mt. Hood by way of Eliot Glacier Cirque Wall. Unpublished manuscript. Courtesy of Wy'east Club.

—— 1981. Interviews with author, 23 July 1981 & 23 Aug. 1984.

McNeil, Fred. 1937. *Wy'east the Mountain.* Portland.

——. 1937. Wy'easters Climb Sandy Cirque Wall. *Journal*, 20 June 1937.

Metzger, Eldon. 1981. Letter to author.

Middle Sister summit registers. 1903-1929, 1952-1961, & 1966-1969. Mazama Library.

Monner, Al. 1938. First Climb Of Sandy Glacier Cirque. *The Wy'east Climber.*

Montgomery, Bernard. 1984. Letters to author, 26 Nov. 1984 & 17 Dec. 1984.

Montgomery, William J. 1984. Letters to author, 20 Nov. 1984, 9 Dec. 1984, & 30 Dec. 1984.

Mount Hood summit registers. 1883-1887, 1888-1891, 1927-1930, 1935-1937, 1937-1939, & 1956-1958. Mazama Library.

Mount, James. 1932. New Trails Up an Old Mountain. Unpublished manuscript. Courtesy of Barry Mount.

Mount Jefferson summit register. 1895-1932. Mazama Library.

Mount Washington summit registers. 1944-1956 & 1956-1965. Courtesy of Mazama Library.

Mount Washington summit register. 1956-1969. Courtesy of Gary Kirk.

Napier, Robert L. 1963. Winter Ascent of the North Sister. *Summit* March:26-27 & 32.

Newspaper unknown. 1913. Climb to Near Top of Mount Jefferson, Record of Ascents Made in 1854 and 1879 Found by Bend Men. Date approximately,

26 July 1913. Oregon Historical Society, Scrapbook 44:144.

Nicolai, Nick. 1969. Warm Springs Couloir: New Route on Mt. Jefferson. *Mazama.*

Nordeen, Emil. 1984. Interview with author, 3 May 1984.

North Sister summit registers. 1910-1933 & 1952-1967. Mazama Library.

North Sister summit register. 1949-1967. Bx 196, Obsidians Inc. Records. Special Collections, Knight Library, Univ. of Oregon.

Olson, Tim. 1989. Interview with author. Spring 1989.

Oregonian. 1887. Summit of Mount Hood Reached by the North Side, 13 Aug. 1887.

———. 1900. Climbed by New Route, 17 Aug. 1900.

———. 1915. Record Made for Scaling of Peak, 10 March 1915.

Oregon State Archives. 1871. Map of Willamette Valley and Cascade Mountain Military Road. Filed 1 Jan. 1871.

Pearce, George J. 1900. An Early Ascent of Mount Jefferson. *Oregonian,* 24 Aug. 1900. See also *Marion County History* 9 (1965-1968): 12-14.

Pearson, Dave. 1945. A New Route on Mt. Washington. *Mazama* .

———. 1985. Interview with author, 12 Jan. 1985.

Pittock, Henry L. 1864. Early Ascents of Mount Hood. *Oregonian,* 6 Aug. 1864.

Pooley, Dick. 1976. Ladd Glacier. *Mazama.*

Prouty, Harley H. 1911. *Sierra Club Bulletin* 53-54.

Ramsey, Jim. 1984. Letter to author, 12 Sept. 1984. Telephone conversation, 26 Feb. 1985.

Rogers, Tom. 1988. Telephone conversation with author.

Salem Statesman. 1903. On Top of Mt. Jefferson, 27 Aug. 1903. Courtesy of Mazama Library.

Schermer, David, 1989. Interview with author.

Scott, John D. 1925. The 1925 North Side Climb of Mt. Jefferson. *Mazama.*

———. 1929. A Traverse of The North Sister. *Mazama.*

———. 1933. Difficult Ascents of Mt. Jefferson. *Mazama*

Sellers, Ronald. 1923. The Conquest of Mt. Washington. *Mazama.*

Sheldrick, Peter. 1965. Letter to Al Weese, 29 Jan. 1965. Courtesy of Nick Dodge.

Sims, Ray. 1934. History of the Obsidian Club of Eugene. Unpublished manuscript. Obsidian Library, Eugene, Oregon.

Spier, Leslie. 1930. *Klamath Ethnography.* Berkeley, Ca., University of California Press.

South Sister summit register. 1930-1952. Bx 196, Obsidians, Inc. Records. Special Collections, Knight Library, University of Oregon.

South Sister summit register. 1930-1939. Mazama Library.

Steck, Allen. 1985. Letter to author, 25 Aug. 1985.

Steel, William Gladstone. 1907. *Steel Points.* I no. 3 (April).

———. 1885-1934. Scrapbooks. Mazama Library.

Stone, W.E. 1917. An Unofficial Ascent of Mt. Jefferson. *Mazama.*

Three Fingered Jack summit registers. 1936-1960 & 1966-1972. Mazama Library.

Wagstaff, David. 1985. Interview with author, 9 Jan. 1985.

Waldo, John Breckenridge. 1880-1907. Letters. Courtesy of Sheila Pilcher. Other letters courtesy of Folger Johnson, Waldo's only grandson. See also Waldo, John Breckenridge. 1985. *Diaries and Letters from the High Cascades of Oregon.* Ed. Gerald W. Williams. USFS publication #R-6-Umpqua-001-1985.

Weygandt, Wesley. 1984. Interview with author, 11 Nov. 1984.

White, Victor H. 1972. *The Story of Lige Coleman.* Sandy, Oregon: St. Paul's Press.

Wickwire, Jim. 1984. Telephone conversation with author, 12 Dec. 1984.

Woods, Don. 1985. Interview with author, 24 Feb. 1985. Letters to author, 2 June 1984 & 31 Aug. 1985.

Woods, George L. 1886. Gold Seeking. *Oregonian,* run serially on June 13, 20, 27, and July 4, 1886. See also, Trail-Making in the Oregon Mountains. *The Overland Monthly* 4, no. 3 (March 1870): 201-213; Victor, Francis Fuller. *All Over Oregon and Washington.* San Francisco. 1872. pp. 311-320: *Oregon Argus,* 8 Aug. 1857.

Young, Del. 1984. Letter to author, 4 June 1984.

Zimmermann, T.C. Price. 1969. North Sister's East Buttress. *Mazama.*

INDEX